THOMAS
AND HENY

MY BIG "I WONDER WHY..." BOOK

KINGFISHER

KINGFISHER
Kingfisher Publications Plc
New Penderel House
283–288 High Holborn
London WC1V 7HZ

Material in this edition previously published by Kingfisher
Publications Plc in the *I Wonder Why* series.

First published in hardback by Kingfisher Publications Plc 1999
10 9 8 7 6 5 4 3 2 1
First published in paperback 2000
10 9 8 7 6 5 4 3 2 1
1TR(PB)/BS/0700/TWP/150SMA
Copyright © Kingfisher Publications Plc 1996

A CIP catalogue record for this book is
available from the British Library.

ISBN 0 7534 0438 9 (hb)
ISBN 0 7534 0565 2 (pb)

Printed in Singapore

Project editor: Clare Oliver
Contributing editors: Brigid Avison, Jackie Gaff,
Claire Llewellyn
Editorial assistant: Virginie Verhague
Indexer: Sue Lightfoot

Cover design: Smiljka Surla
***I Wonder Why* series designer:** David West Children's Books
Additional design: Smiljka Surla
Art editor: Christina Fraser
Picture referencing: Amanda Francis

Publishing director: Jim Miles

Production manager: Susan Latham

Contributing authors: Brigid Avison; Andrew Charman;
Anita Ganeri; Christopher Maynard; Richard Mead; Clare
Oliver; Amanda O'Neill; Josephine Paker; Steve
Parker; Philip Steele; Carole Stott; Barbara
Taylor; Rod Theodorou; Brenda Walpole;
Jenny Wood

Contributing consultants:
Andrew Branson; British
Museum: Department of
Egyptian Antiquities and Department
of Graeco-Roman Antiquites; Michael
Chinery; Eryl Davies; Dougal Dixon;
Ian Graham; David Haycock, Paul
Hillyard; Dr David Hughes; Keith Lye;
Dr Elizabeth McCall Smith; Geoff
Puplett; Dr Peter Rowan; Peter Thoms

CONTENTS

THE UNIVERSE AND PLANET EARTH

8 What is the universe?
8 When did it begin?
9 Will the universe ever end?
10 What is the Milky Way?
11 How many stars are there?
12 How hot is the Sun?
13 Will the Sun ever go out?
14 How many planets are there?
15 What's the difference between stars and planets?
16 Is the Earth round?
17 What is the Earth made of?
18 How old is the Earth?
19 Has the Earth changed much?
20 Where are the highest mountains?
21 Can mountains shrink?
22 Which mountains breathe fire?
23 Do people live on volcanoes?
24 How high is the sky?
24 What is the greenhouse effect?
26 What are clouds made of?
26 When does rain fall from clouds?

27 How cold is snow?
28 Where do thunderstorms start?
29 What is thunder?
30 How big is the ocean?
31 Which is the biggest ocean?
31 What's the difference between a sea and an ocean?
32 What makes waves roll?

SCIENCE AND THE HUMAN BODY

34 What is science about?
35 What do scientists do?
36 Why do I run out of energy?
37 What is energy?
38 Why does the spoon get hot when I stir my cocoa?
38 Why is sunlight warm?
39 How do hang-gliders hitch lifts?
40 What is sound?
41 Why do trumpeters blow raspberries?
41 Can sound travel under water?
42 What is air made of?
43 How do bubbles get into fizzy drinks?
43 Why do cakes rise?
44 Why do shadows happen?
45 Why can I see through glass?
46 Can light bounce?
47 Why do my legs look shorter under water?

48 Why do rainbows happen?

49 Why is grass green?

49 Can cats see in colour?

50 Why do we need air?

51 Why do we need light?

51 Why do we need water?

52 Where do I come from?

53 What is my tummy button?

54 How many bones do I have?

55 What is my funny bone?

56 How do I move?

56 Why do strong people have big muscles?

57 What is cramp?

58 What does my heart do?

59 What is blood for?

59 How big is my heart?

60 What is inside my head?

61 What makes me feel things?

62 Why do I breathe?

63 What makes me hiccup?

63 What makes me sneeze?

64 Why do I blink?

65 Why can't I see in the dark?

66 Why are ears such a funny shape?

66 Why do I feel dizzy when I spin around?

68 What is my nose for?

69 What is my tongue for?

69 Why do teeth fall out?

70 Why do I get ill sometimes?

TRANSPORT AND BUILDINGS

72 Which is the fastest car?

72 Which is the fastest boat?

73 Which is the fastest plane?

74 Why do cars need petrol?

75 What happens inside car engines?

76 Why don't ships sink?

76 How do submarines sink?

77 Which ships fly?

78 What are houses made from?

80 Why do houses need holes?

81 What do diggers do?

82 How are bridges built?

83 Do bridges sway about in the wind?

84 Which bridge can break in two?

INVENTIONS

86 Why do people invent things?

87 Is everything invented?

87 Where do inventors get their ideas?

88 Why does my watch tick?
88 How did people manage before clocks?
89 How does a grandfather keep good time?
90 What were the first cars like?
90 How do you ride on air?
91 Which bikes have sails?
92 How can you fit 1,000 books in your pocket?
93 Which computer was as big as a bus?
93 Who was Mr Biro?
94 Why does the telephone ring?
95 How can glass link the world?
95 Are phone lines just for voices?
96 How can you fight a hungry dinosaur?

HISTORY

98 How long ago did dinosaurs live?
99 How many dinosaurs were there?
100 What happened to the dinosaurs?
101 Are there any dinosaurs around today?
102 Why do we call Egyptians ancient?
103 Why were the Egyptians great?
104 Who were the Ancient Greeks?
105 How did Greece grow bigger and bigger?
106 Who were the Romans?

107 Did all the Romans live in Rome?
108 Where can you visit Ancient Rome?
109 How do we know about the Romans?
110 What were the Middle Ages in the middle of?
112 Why did castles have moats?
114 Who made a new home in the New World?
115 Who built the best home for the next world?
116 Who was the 'last' king of France?
117 Who was the first president of the United States?
118 Who steamed into the twentieth century?

COUNTRIES AND PEOPLES

120 What is a country?
121 Why do countries fly flags?
122 Which country has the most people?
123 Which is the biggest country?
123 Where is there land but no countries?
124 Where are there only two seasons?
125 Where does it pour for a month?
126 Who rides on a snowmobile?

127 Where do you park your bike
  in China?
127 Who paints pictures on trucks?
128 Who writes with a paintbrush?
128 Who reads back-to-front?
129 Which country speaks over
  800 languages?
130 Where are wheatfields bigger
  than countries?
131 Where does chocolate grow
  on trees?
131 Which country has more sheep
  than people?
132 Who lights the lamps at
  New Year?
132 Who brings in the New Year
  with a bang?
133 Who blows a horn at New Year?
134 Where do elephants glow in
  the dark?
134 When do people eat green food?
135 When is the Day of the Dead?
136 Could people live
  in space?

143 ...and between monkeys
  and apes?
143 ...and rabbits and hares?
144 Why do animals have skeletons
  inside their bodies?
145 Which animals have skeletons
  on the outside?
146 Do reptiles have skin like ours?
147 Why do snakes shed
  their skin?
147 Why do some lizards
  have horns and spikes?
148 Why do birds
  have feathers?
148 Which bird can
  fly backwards?
149 Why can't penguins fly?
150 What is an insect?
150 When is a fly not a fly?
151 What is a bug?
151 Are spiders insects?
152 Why do caterpillars change
  into butterflies?
154 How do fish breathe
  under water?
154 How do fish swim?
155 Which bird flies under water?
155 Which animal is jet-propelled?

ANIMALS

139 Which is the
  biggest animal?
140 What's the difference
  between sharks
  and dolphins?
142 What's the difference
  between frogs and
  toads?
142 ...and alligators and
  crocodiles?

INDEX

THE UNIVERSE AND THE EARTH

What is the universe?

The whole world and everything beyond it is the universe. It is all the stars and planets, the Earth and its plants and animals, you and me – everything.

● You are made of the same stuff as a star!

● There are huge groups of stars in space. They're called galaxies, and they're like gigantic star-cities.

● The Big Bang explosion sent the young universe flying out in all directions. Over vast ages of time, bits came together to make galaxies.

● The galaxies are still speeding apart today, and the universe is getting bigger.

When did it begin?

Many astronomers think that everything in the universe was once packed together in one small lump. Then, about 15 billion years ago, there was a gigantic explosion which they call the Big Bang.

● To see how the universe is getting bigger, watch the spots as you blow up a spotty balloon.

Will the universe ever end?

Some astronomers think the universe will just carry on getting bigger as the galaxies speed apart. Others think that the galaxies may one day start falling back towards each other until they crash together in a Big Crunch!

● Astronomers are scientists who study the stars and the planets.

● No one knows where all the material to make the universe came from in the first place.

What is the Milky Way?

The Milky Way is the galaxy we live in. It is made up of all the stars you can see in the sky at night, and lots and lots more you can't see.

• The Milky Way is a spiral galaxy. Below you can see what it looks like from above – a bit like a whirlpool with long spiralling arms.

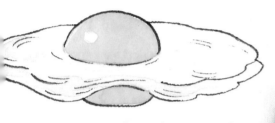

• From the side, a spiral galaxy looks like two fried eggs stuck together.

• The Milky Way got its name because at night we can sometimes see part of it looking like a band of milky white light across the sky.

• We live on a planet called Earth, which travels around a star called the Sun.

10

● Astronomers usually give galaxies numbers instead of names. Only a few have names that tell us what they look like – the Whirlpool, the Sombrero, and the Black Eye, for example!

● These are the three main galaxy shapes.

Irregular (no special shape)

Elliptical (egg-shaped)

Spiral

How many stars are there?

There are about 1000 billion stars in the Milky Way. That's nearly 200 stars for every person living on Earth today!

Although we can't see all of it, astronomers have worked out how big the universe is and how many stars it has. There are about 100 billion billion stars, in around 100 billion galaxies. It's hard even to think about so many stars, let alone count them!

How hot is the Sun?

Like all stars, our Sun is a huge ball of super-hot gas. It is hottest in the middle – the temperature there is around 15 million °C.

The outside of the Sun is a lot cooler than the middle – only 6000 °C. But this is still 25 times hotter than the hottest kitchen oven!

● Dark patches called sunspots come and go on the face of the Sun. They make it look as though it has chickenpox. Sunspots are dark because they are cooler and so give out less light than the rest of the Sun.

● Most sunspots are larger than the Earth.

● Plants and animals couldn't live without the Sun's heat and light.

● The Sun is the only star that's close enough to Earth for us to feel its heat. The next nearest star to Earth is called Proxima Centauri. Our Sun's light takes 8.3 minutes to reach us, but Proxima Centauri's takes 4.3 years!

● The Sun uses more than 30 million truck loads of fuel every second!

Will the Sun ever go out?

One day the Sun will use up all its gas fuel and die. But this won't happen in your lifetime, or your children's, or even your great-great-great grandchildren's! Astronomers think that the Sun has enough gas fuel to last for at least another 5 billion years.

How many planets are there?

Our planet, the Earth, has eight neighbours. Together they make a family of nine planets which travel around the Sun. We call the Sun, and all the space bodies that whirl around it, the solar system.

Besides the Sun and the planets, the solar system includes moons, mini-planets called asteroids, and comets.

● Comets are rather like huge dirty snowballs. Most stay out on the edge of the solar system, but a few travel close to the Sun. These comets grow gas and dust tails, millions of kilometres long, when the Sun's heat starts to melt them.

● The word planet comes from the Greek word *planetes*, which means wanderer.

Mars

Mercury   Venus   Earth

Jupiter

Sun

Planet   Orbit

- An orbit is the path of a planet around the Sun, or a moon around a planet. The planets all have different orbits. Mercury is the closest planet to the Sun. Pluto is usually the farthest away.

- Millions of asteroids orbit the Sun, in a belt between Mars and Jupiter. Some are like grains of sand. Others are as big as houses. A few are the size of England!

What's the difference between stars and planets?

The planets aren't as big or as hot as stars, and they can't make light of their own. They were made from the leftovers of the same gas and dust cloud that gave birth to our star, the Sun.

Saturn

Uranus

Neptune

Pluto

Is the Earth round?

If you were an astronaut floating about in space, the Earth would look like a gigantic ball. It isn't perfectly round, though. Like a ball that's been gently squashed, it's slightly flatter at the top and bottom, and it bulges out just a little at the middle.

Equator

● The Earth measures 40,075 kilometres around its 'waist' – the equator. If you walked night and day, it would take you more than a year to get this far!

● The Earth looks blue from space. That's because nearly three-quarters of it is covered by the sea.

The crust is the rocky layer beneath your feet.

The mantle is a thick layer of rock. It's so hot that some of the rock has melted.

The core is made of metal. The outer core is runny and liquid, but the inner core is solid.

Outer core

Inner core

● It's very hot indeed at the centre of the Earth – more than 5000 °C. That's about 150 times hotter than a really scorching hot summer's day!

What is the Earth made of?

The Earth is made up of different layers of rock and metal. Some of the layers are hard, but others are so hot that they've melted and are runny – a bit like hot sticky toffee.

● The Earth's crust doesn't stop at the seashore. It goes on under the deepest oceans.

How old is the Earth?

Scientists think the Earth formed about 4,600 million years ago – although no one was there to see! They think the Moon formed then, too.

● Human beings are very new to the Earth. If you imagine our planet's 4600-million-year-long history squeezed into one year, people have only been around since late on 31 December!

▽ About 200 million years ago there was just one super-continent called Pangaea.

Pangaea

△ About 180 million years ago Pangaea began to break up.

● Continents are massive pieces of land. There are seven of them in all. Trace them from a map, and try to see how they once fitted together.

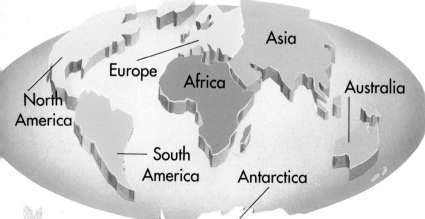

Asia

Europe

Africa

Australia

North America

South America

Antarctica

● Emus live in Australia, rheas in South America, and ostriches in Africa. They look similar, and none of them can fly. They may have been related to one kind of bird. It could have walked to all three continents millions of years ago, when the land was joined.

▽ About 65 million years ago the continents drifted farther apart.

Has the Earth changed much?

Yes, it has! About 300 million years ago, most of the land was joined together in one big piece. Then it began to break up into smaller pieces called continents. These slowly drifted apart, until they reached the places they're in today.

▽ Today, the continents are still drifting.

● North America and Europe are still moving apart by about 4 centimetres each year. That's about the length of your thumb.

Where are the highest mountains?

● Himalaya means 'home of the snows'. It's a good name for these freezing peaks.

The Himalayas in Asia are the world's highest mountains. They're so high that they're known as 'the roof of the world'. The towering mountain peaks are bitterly cold places, where the snow and ice never melt.

● These are the highest mountains in each continent:

Asia – Mt Everest 8848 m

S. America – Aconcagua 6959 m

N. America – Mt McKinley 6194 m

Africa – Mt Kilimanjaro 5895 m

Europe – Mt Elbrus 5633 m

Antarctica – Vinson Massif 5139 m

Australia – Mt Kosciusko 2230 m

Can mountains shrink?

Many mountains are getting smaller all the time. Every day, small chips of rock are carried away by ice, snow and running water.

Some mountains are getting bigger, though. The Himalayas are still being pushed up by movements inside the Earth.

● In Hawaii there is a mountain called Mauna Kea which is more than 1,300 metres higher than Mount Everest. Most of it is under the sea, though.

● The higher you go up a mountain, the colder it becomes. Many of the animals that live high up on mountains have thick woolly coats to keep out the cold – goats, llamas and yaks, for example.

Which mountains breathe fire?

Volcanoes are mountains that sometimes spurt out burning ash, gas, and hot runny rock called lava. The gas and fiery lava come from deep down inside the Earth, and burst up through cracks in the crust.

● The saucer-like top of a volcano is called a crater. Sometimes a dead volcano's crater fills with rainwater and makes a beautiful lake.

● There are about 500 active volcanoes on land. There are even more under the sea.

Do people live on volcanoes?

It's a risky thing to do, but many people live on volcanoes – especially farmers. The ash from a volcano makes the soil very rich, so the farmers can grow bumper crops. They need to be able to run fast, though!

● There are volcanoes in space, too. Olympus Mons on the planet Mars is three times higher than Earth's Mount Everest.

● Pilots beware! The ash and dust from a volcano can get inside a plane's engines and stop them dead.

How high is the sky?

The sky is part of an invisible skin of air around the Earth. This skin is called the atmosphere, and it reaches out into space for about 500 kilometres.

There's a very important gas called oxygen in the atmosphere – we all need to breathe oxygen to stay alive.

● The Earth is the only planet known to have enough oxygen for living things.

● If the Earth gets too hot, the ice at the Poles could melt. The seas would rise and drown many towns along the coasts.

What is the greenhouse effect?

The greenhouse effect is the name scientists have given to a hot problem. Waste gases from factories, power stations and cars are building up in the atmosphere and trapping too much heat close to the Earth. Our planet is slowly getting warmer – like a greenhouse in summer.

OZONE LAYER

3 Above the planes is the ozone layer. This works a bit like a sunblock, protecting us from the Sun's burning rays.

2 Planes fly in the next layer, high above the clouds where the skies are clear. The air is thinner here, and has less oxygen in it.

1 The atmosphere is made up of different layers. In the lowest layer, the air carries clouds and weather around the Earth.

What are clouds made of?

Some clouds look like they're made of cotton wool – but they're not! Clouds are made of billions of water droplets and ice crystals. These are so tiny and light that they float in the air.

● You'd need your umbrella on Mount Wai-'ale-'ale in Hawaii. It rains there for 350 days each year.

● Without rain, no plants would grow. Then what would we all eat?

When does rain fall from clouds?

Rain falls when water droplets in a cloud start joining together. They get bigger and heavier until, in the end, they are too heavy to float, and fall to the ground as rain.

• Have you ever heard of showers of frogs or fish? Well, they do happen. The animals are sometimes sucked up from ponds by extra-strong winds. Later on, they fall to the ground with the rain.

How cold is snow?

Snowflakes are water droplets that have frozen into crystals of ice. To stay frozen, they have to be at freezing point – that's 0 °C. If they get any warmer than this, snowflakes melt and fall to the ground as rain.

• The biggest snowman ever built was more than 22 metres high. That's about as tall as a seven-storey building.

Where do thunderstorms start?

Thunderstorms start in the huge black thunderclouds that sometimes gather at the end of a hot summer's day. Inside the clouds, strong winds hurl the water droplets around, and the cloud crackles with electricity. It flashes through the sky in great dazzling sparks, which we call lightning.

- It's safest to stay inside during a thunderstorm. Never shelter under a tree – it might get struck by lightning.

- An American man was struck by lightning seven times! Roy C. Sullivan had his hair set alight twice and his eyebrows burnt off. He even lost a big toenail.

- Lightning can travel as far as 140,000 kilometres in 1 second flat!

● To find out how far away a storm is, count the number of seconds between the lightning and the thunder. The storm is 1 kilometre away for every 3 seconds you count.

● The biggest thunderclouds tower 16 kilometres into the air. That's nearly twice the height of Mount Everest.

What is thunder?

Sparks of lightning are incredibly hot. As they flash through the sky, they heat the air so quickly that it makes a loud booming noise like an explosion. This is thunder.

How big is the ocean?

The ocean is truly ENORMOUS! It covers more than twice as much of the Earth as land does. In fact, it's made up of four oceans – the Pacific, the Atlantic, the Indian and the Arctic. Although these all have different names, they flow into each other to make one huge world ocean.

● Don't go for a swim in the Arctic Ocean. It's the coldest of the oceans, and for most of the year it's covered in ice.

Which is the biggest ocean?

The Pacific is by far the biggest ocean in the world. It's larger than the other three oceans put together, and it's also much deeper. If you look at a globe, you'll see that the Pacific reaches halfway around the world.

These drops of water show the oceans in order of size.

Pacific

Atlantic

Indian

Arctic

What's the difference between a sea and an ocean?

People often use the words sea and ocean to mean the same thing. That's fine, but to a scientist, seas are just part of an ocean – the parts that are nearest to land. The Mediterranean Sea is between Africa and Europe, for example.

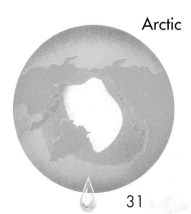

31

What makes waves roll?

● Make your own waves in a bowl of water. The harder you blow across the surface, the bigger the waves.

Waves are ripples of water blown across the surface of the ocean by the wind. On a calm day they hardly move, but in stormy weather they roll faster and faster, and grow higher and higher, until they form huge walls of water.

● Some waves are called white horses because their curly white tips look like horses' manes.

● At Waimea Bay, Hawaii, surfers ride waves up to 10 metres high – that's six times taller than a man!

SCIENCE
AND THE
HUMAN BODY

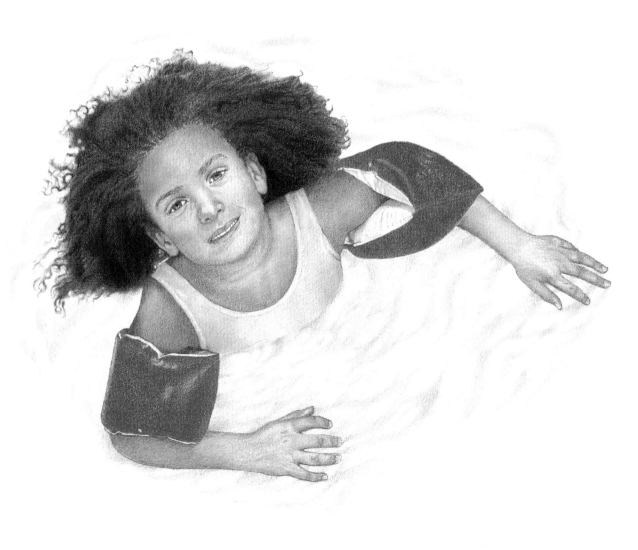

What is science about?

Science is all about discovering how and why things happen in the world around you. It's about everyday things like finding out where water goes when it boils, as well as more complicated things like why we need water to live.

3 Put some water in the freezer and leave it for an hour or two. What do you notice when you take it out? The water isn't liquid any more – it's a solid, and you can't pour solids.

2 Now fill a jug with water and pour it into a cup. Most liquids will pour, but some move faster than others. Try pouring some honey into a saucer – does it move as quickly as water?

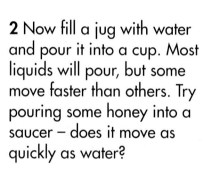

1 The kitchen is a great place for scientists. Start by turning on a tap and looking at the water that flows out. Runny things like water are called liquids.

What do scientists do?

One of the first things scientists do is to ask questions. Then they try to answer the questions by looking closely at things and testing out their ideas. We call this experimenting. Scientists sometimes manage to come up with the answers – but not always!

4 All liquids can change shape, but most solids can't. Pour some water into a jelly mould and it will fill up all the nooks and crannies. What happens when you put ice cubes in?

5 Ask a grown-up to put a cup of water into a saucepan and boil it for you for 5 minutes. Lots of steam comes off, doesn't it? Let the water cool, then pour it back into the cup. There's less water now – where has the rest gone?

6 When water boils, it changes from a liquid into a gas called water vapour. We can't see this gas, so it looks as though the water has disappeared.

35

Why do I run out of energy?

● When you run, the stored energy in your body is changed into movement energy.

You run out of energy because you use it! Walking, running and jumping all need energy – without it you wouldn't be able to talk, write, read or even sleep! Energy is stored inside your body and comes from your food. That's why you get hungry – your body is telling you to put back some of the energy you've used.

● Lots of things give out energy, in many different forms. Here are just some of them.

Fire = heat energy

Bike = movement energy

Drum = sound energy

● Eating a small apple gives you enough energy to sleep for half an hour.

● Energy is never made or destroyed. It just changes from one form to another. Bending a bow stores energy in the bow. This changes into movement energy as the arrow flies from the bow.

What is energy?

Energy makes things happen – nothing in the universe would work without it. You can't see energy, but you can see what it does to things around you. Because of energy, cars move and planes fly, lamps give out light, drums make music, and fires give off heat.

Food = chemical energy

Train = electrical energy

Torch = light energy

Why does the spoon get hot when I stir my cocoa?

Heat energy never stays still. It is always moving. The teaspoon warms up when you stir your cocoa because heat energy is moving from the hot drink into the spoon.

● Things that allow heat to pass through them easily are called conductors. A metal spoon is a good conductor.

● Our bodies give off heat all the time. Some burglar alarms work by picking up the heat given off by a burglar's body.

Why is sunlight warm?

Sunlight is warm because the Sun gives off heat as well as light energy. The Sun's heat energy travels towards us in invisible straight lines called heat rays. You can't see them, of course, but you can feel them on your skin on hot sunny days.

● You get cold feet when you stand on a tiled floor because the tiles carry heat energy away from them. Your feet feel warmer on a carpet because it doesn't carry heat away as well as the tiles do.

How do hang-gliders hitch lifts?

When the Sun heats the land, the land then warms the air above it. Warm air is lighter than cold air, and it rises up into the sky. Hang-gliders use this rising warm air to help them to fly. The rising currents of warm air are called thermals.

What is sound?

Sound is a type of energy. It happens when something shakes or moves back and forwards really quickly. The shaking movements are called vibrations. You hear sounds because vibrations travel through the air into your ears.

● Some singers can sing a note which is so high and so loud that it breaks a glass!

● Here's a way to see how sounds vibrate. Tie a piece of thread to some tissue paper. Now, put on some loud music and hold the thread in front of a loud-speaker. The vibrations should make the tissue paper shake. If they don't, turn up the music!

● Crashing a pair of cymbals together makes them vibrate, sending out ringing sounds.

40

Why do trumpeters blow raspberries?

Blowing raspberries is the only way to get sounds out of a trumpet! It makes a trumpeter's lips vibrate, and this makes the air inside the trumpet shake, too. The air comes out the other end as a musical note!

● Sound travels through air at 340 metres per second. That's nearly the length of four football pitches.

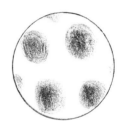

Can sound travel under water?

● Sound needs something to travel through – air, water, or some other material. There's no air in space, so astronauts have to use radios to talk to one another.

Yes, it can! Sound moves four times faster through water than through air. It can travel such long distances that whales can hear each other when they are over a hundred kilometres apart.

What is air made of?

Air is a mixture of gases – mostly nitrogen and oxygen, with a little bit of carbon dioxide and some water vapour. It also has tiny bits of salt, dust and dirt. You can't see, smell or taste the air, but you can feel it when the wind blows.

● You're using air when you take a deep breath and blow out the candles on a cake!

● We don't notice it, but the air around us is heavy, and pushes down on us. The air in a medium-sized room weighs as much as 70 cans of baked beans!

42

How do bubbles get into fizzy drinks?

The bubbles in fizzy drinks are made of carbon dioxide. The gas is squashed into the bottle so hard that it disappears into the drink. When the bottle is opened, the bubbles have room to escape and start fizzing into the air.

● Make your own bubbles of carbon dioxide gas by adding a teaspoon of baking powder to a beaker of water. Stand by for the fizz!

Why do cakes rise?

When you put a cake in the oven, the mixture heats up and makes bubbles of carbon dioxide. These grow bigger in the heat, and make the cake rise.

● The air you beat into a cake mixture also helps to make the cake deliciously light.

Why do shadows happen?

Light travels in straight lines called rays. When the rays hit something that they can't shine through, the light is blocked, and a dark shadow forms on the other side.

● There are lots of things that light can't shine through – walls, furniture, your own body, for example. We call these things opaque.

● Try to make animal shadows on a wall by wiggling your fingers in the beam of a bright torch.

● Light is another kind of energy. Plants use the energy in sunlight to make food for themselves in their leaves. Sunflowers get all the sunlight they can by turning to face the Sun as it moves across the sky.

● Did you know that you can use shadows to tell the time? Next time it's sunny, stand a pencil inside a cotton reel on a piece of paper. Every hour, draw a line along the pencil's shadow, and write down the time. Now you can use your shadow clock to tell the time on every sunny day.

Why can I see through glass?

You can see through glass because it's transparent – that means it's clear, and it lets the light shine through. Glass is great for windows because it lets sunlight into a room, and allows you to see what's going on in the world outside!

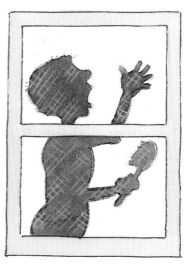

● Bathroom windows are often made of frosted glass. This still lets some light through, but the frosting stops people from seeing straight through the glass.

Can light bounce?

When rays of light hit something that they can't shine through, they bounce off it – just like a ball bouncing off the ground. This is called reflection. We are able to see things because light is reflected off them into our eyes.

● You can see yourself when you look down into a puddle because the smooth water reflects the light straight back into your eyes.

● Up periscope! A submarine officer looks through a periscope to see what's happening above the water. Mirrors inside the periscope reflect light from things above the water straight down into the officer's eyes.

● The Moon reflects light from the Sun. It has no light of its own.

● See what happens when light passes through a single drop of water. Cut a hole in a piece of card and stick clear tape over the top. Carefully put a drop of water on the tape and look through it at something small, like a ladybird. It will make it look bigger.

Why do my legs look shorter under water?

When light enters water, its rays travel more slowly than they do through the air. This changes the way we see things. Looking down through the water in a swimming pool, your legs look very short and dumpy. Don't worry – they aren't really!

● As light passes through water, it changes the way we see things. This makes it tricky to net fish – they aren't where they appear to be. To catch one, you have to aim below the place where you actually see it.

Why do rainbows happen?

Although sunlight looks white, it's really made up of lots of different colours. During a shower of rain, the Sun sometimes shines through the tiny raindrops that fall through the air. When this happens, the water makes the light spread into all its different colours. The colours always appear in the same order, and a beautiful rainbow forms in the sky.

Card

Torch beam

Reflected light

Mirror

● Another way to see a rainbow is to hold a mirror in a shallow dish of water. Try to bounce sunlight or torchlight off the mirror on to a piece of white card. The water should make the light spread out into a rainbow.

● You don't have to wait for rain to see a rainbow. Water the garden on a sunny day, and you may see rainbow colours in the spray.

Why is grass green?

We see things when light reflects off them into our eyes. But not all of white light's colours are reflected. Some are soaked up. Grass looks green because it soaks up all the colours in white light apart from green.

● The bright colours of many animals often work as a warning. The black and yellow stripes on a wasp warn us – and other animals – to keep away from its poisonous sting.

Can cats see in colour?

● Many animals don't really need to see in colour. They rely far more on their sharp hearing and sense of smell.

Yes, they can – but they don't see all the colours that you do! Cats don't really need to see bright colours, as most of them are busiest at night, outdoors hunting for food.

Why do we need air?

All the animals on Earth need to breathe the oxygen in air to stay alive – and that includes you! That's because bodies use oxygen to make energy for living and growing.

● All plants need air, light and water to live and grow. So do people, and every other living thing on our planet.

● Even though they live in the sea, whales breathe oxygen from the air. Sperm whales can hold their breath for up to two hours before coming up for air.

Why do we need light?

Without the Sun's light, there would be nothing to eat! Plants are the only living things that can make their own food, and they need sunlight to do this. Everything else on Earth feeds on plants, or on plant-eating animals. If there weren't any plants, we'd all starve to death!

Why do we need water?

It's hard to imagine, but more than two-thirds of your body is made of water. And the same is true for most other animals and plants. All of the living things on Earth need water to stay alive. Without it, they would die.

● You can survive for many weeks without food. But without water you'd last just three or four days.

Where do I come from?

You began when a tiny egg inside your mother (no bigger than a full stop) joined with a tiny bit of your father, called a sperm. Then you grew and grew until you were big enough to be born.

- You stayed in your mother's womb for about nine months. As you got bigger, her womb stretched to make space for you.

Womb

Sperm

Egg

- This is what an egg surrounded by lots of sperm looks like under a microscope.

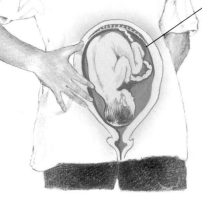

Womb

- In the womb, you floated in a kind of bag filled with water which kept you safe and warm.

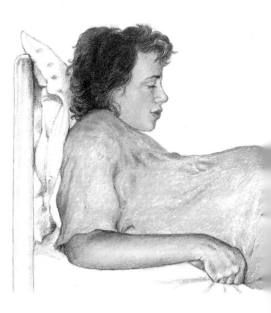

- You grew inside your mother in a part of her body called the womb.

- When you were ready to be born, the opening of your mother's womb stretched to let you out.

52

Umbilical cord – the tube that joined you to your mother.

● As soon as you were born, you took a big gulp of air and started breathing.

What is my tummy button?

Your tummy button is the place where a special tube joined you to your mother before you were born. The tube had blood vessels in it, so your mother's blood could bring you oxygen and food to keep you alive and growing while you were in her womb. You didn't need her blood after you were born, so the tube was cut.

● After lots of hard pushing, you popped out of your mother's body through a hole between her legs called her vagina.

53

How many bones do I have?

When you were born, you had about 350 bones. But by the time you finish growing, you will have just over 200!

The missing bones won't have fallen out or disappeared. Instead, as you get older, some of your smaller bones will join together to make bigger ones.

- Without bones inside you to give you a shape, you'd be like a floppy, squishy bag.

Thigh bone

- The longest bone in your body is the one above your knee, called your thigh bone.

- Your bones are partly made of a hard stony stuff called calcium, but unlike stones they are alive. They get bigger as you grow up.

Foot bones

- Most of us have twelve pairs of ribs, but some people have an extra one. Your ribs help to keep your lungs and heart safe.

- Although your skull is made of lots of bones, most of them are fixed together. Only your jaw bone moves.

- Bones are hard and strong. They help to keep the softer parts inside you (like your brain) from getting hurt.

Breast bone

Ribs

Backbone

Hip bones

Skull

Arm bones

Hand bones

What is my funny bone?

The funny thing about your funny bone is that it isn't a bone at all. It's a nerve that runs just under your skin over each elbow. If you bang your elbow, the nerve is banged, too. It sends a message to your brain and you feel pain!

How do I move?

Muscles make you move, by pulling your bones about. When you smile or cry, speak or eat, walk or skip, muscles are doing the work.

● A muscle can only make itself shorter. It needs another muscle pulling the other way to stretch it out again.

● Your biggest muscles are the ones you sit on!

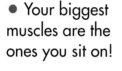

Why do strong people have big muscles?

● Many tennis players have bigger muscles in the arm they use to hold their racket.

Muscles get bigger and stronger if they are used a lot. That's why sportswomen and men practise hard and do lots of exercises.

• To make a bone move, a muscle gets shorter. This pulls the bone one way. To pull the bone back again, another muscle gets shorter. Muscles are fixed to your bones by strong white strings called tendons.

Tendon

This muscle tightens to bend your arm.

When this muscle tightens, your arm straightens.

What is cramp?

Cramp is when a muscle suddenly feels tight and painful. It stops moving properly and it feels like it's stuck. No one is quite sure why cramp happens, but it goes away if you rest the sore part. Rubbing it can also help.

• Have you ever had a stitch after running? It's a pain in your middle, just under your ribs. It means you've got cramp in the breathing muscle below your lungs.

What does my heart do?

Your heart is a very special muscle which keeps blood moving around your body. If you put your hand on your chest near your heart, you'll feel it beating. Each time it beats, it pumps blood out around your body.

● To hear a heart beating, find somewhere quiet and rest your ear against a friend's chest. You should hear two sounds close together – 'lub-dub', 'lub-dub', 'lub-dub'.

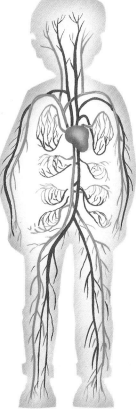

● Blood travels round your body in thin tubes called blood vessels.

● Your body is using up oxygen all the time, keeping you alive, so it has to keep getting more from your lungs.

Blood from your head

To the body

Blood from your body

- One side of your heart pumps blood to your lungs to get oxygen. The other side pumps it around your body.

Blood to your lungs

Blood from your lungs

Blood with oxygen

Blood without oxygen

What is blood for?

Your blood is like a fast-moving river flowing around your body. It carries useful things – like oxygen from the air you breathe, and the goodness from the food you eat – to every part of you. It also helps your body to fight germs.

- When you were a baby, you had less than a litre of blood – not quite enough to fill a milk carton. When you grow up, you will have about five litres of blood – enough to half fill a bucket!

- Some insects have blue or green blood.

How big is my heart?

Our hearts grow with us – they get bigger as we do. Whatever size you are now, your heart will be a bit bigger than your fist.

59

What is inside my head?

The most exciting and important part of your body is hidden inside your head, beneath your hair, your skin and your hard skull bone. It is your brain.

Your brain is the part of you that thinks and remembers. It also makes sure the rest of your body is doing what it should!

● Your brain has two sides. The right side of your brain looks after the left side of your body, while the left side looks after the right side of your body.

● People's brains come in different sizes. But bigger brains don't make people more clever – any more than having big feet makes them better runners!

• Nerves tell your body what's happening to it – like whether water feels too hot or too cold.

• Messages travel very fast along your nerves. The quickest go as fast as 400 km/h!

• Your nerves start in your brain, then travel in a thick bundle down your back (inside your backbone). From there they branch out to every part of your body.

What makes me feel things?

Every minute of the day your brain is being sent messages about all the different things that are happening inside and outside your body. Some are about things you feel. All the messages travel to your brain along paths called nerves.

• Hurt or pain are feelings that tell you if something is wrong. They are your body's warning system. It hurts when you stub your toe because your body is telling you to stop – something is in your way!

Why do I breathe?

You pull air into your body when you breathe. And air is something your body cannot do without, even for just a few minutes.

This is because air has a gas called oxygen in it, and your body needs oxygen to live and grow.

● When you breathe in, air goes down your windpipe to your lungs. These are like big sponges which hold air instead of water.

Windpipe

Lungs

● If you fold your arms across your chest and breathe in, you'll feel your lungs getting bigger as they fill up with air.

What makes me hiccup?

There's a big muscle below your lungs which helps you to breathe. It's called your diaphragm muscle. You hiccup when something makes this muscle pull down really hard, drawing lots of air into your lungs. To stop too much air rushing in, a flap at the top of your windpipe clamps down. This closes off the air flow so quickly that your whole body jerks.

- 'HIC' is air rushing in.

- 'CUP' is the flap clamping down over your windpipe.

What makes me sneeze?

If dust or germs get into your nose, your body makes you sneeze to get rid of them. Your lungs shoot air out, clearing your nose.

- When you sneeze, air rushes down your nose at over 160 kilometres per hour!

Why do I blink?

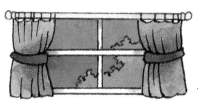

Your eyes make tears all the time, not only when you cry. Blinking spreads the tears across your eyes and stops them from drying out and getting sore.

● The iris is the coloured part of your eye. It works rather like curtains on a window – when it's too dark to see, the iris opens to let in more light. When the light is too bright, the iris tightens up to protect the eye.

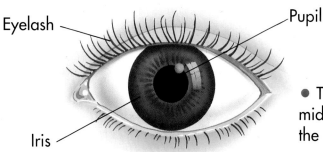

● A blink lasts for about one-third of a second. You do it thousands of times a day.

Eyelash ─ Pupil

Iris

● Eyelashes help to stop things like dust and grit getting into your eyes.

● The black hole in the middle of the eye is called the pupil.

- Jelly-like stuff in your eyeball keeps it in shape, like air in a balloon.

Why can't I see in the dark?

You can't see much when it's dark, because eyes need light to see. If you look at your eyes in a mirror, you'll see a black hole in the middle of them. Light bounces off everything around you and in through this hole. Messages are then sent from your eyes to your brain, telling you what you are looking at.

- The lining at the back of the eye is called the retina. The picture that forms here is upside down! Your brain turns it the right way up.

A nerve inside here carries messages to your brain.

- There's a lens at the front of the eye. It makes sure the things you see aren't fuzzy, by making light shine in the right place at the back of the eye.

Why are ears such a funny shape?

The shape of your ears helps them to catch sounds from the air. The sounds then go through your ear hole into the hidden part of your ear, inside your head. Animals like rabbits can move their ears to help them catch sounds.

Why do I feel dizzy when I spin round?

Inside each ear, you have three loop-shaped tubes with watery liquid in them. This swishes about when you spin round. Special nerves pick up this movement and tell your brain you are spinning. If you stop suddenly, the liquid still swishes about for a bit. Your brain gets the wrong message and you feel dizzy!

Ear lobe

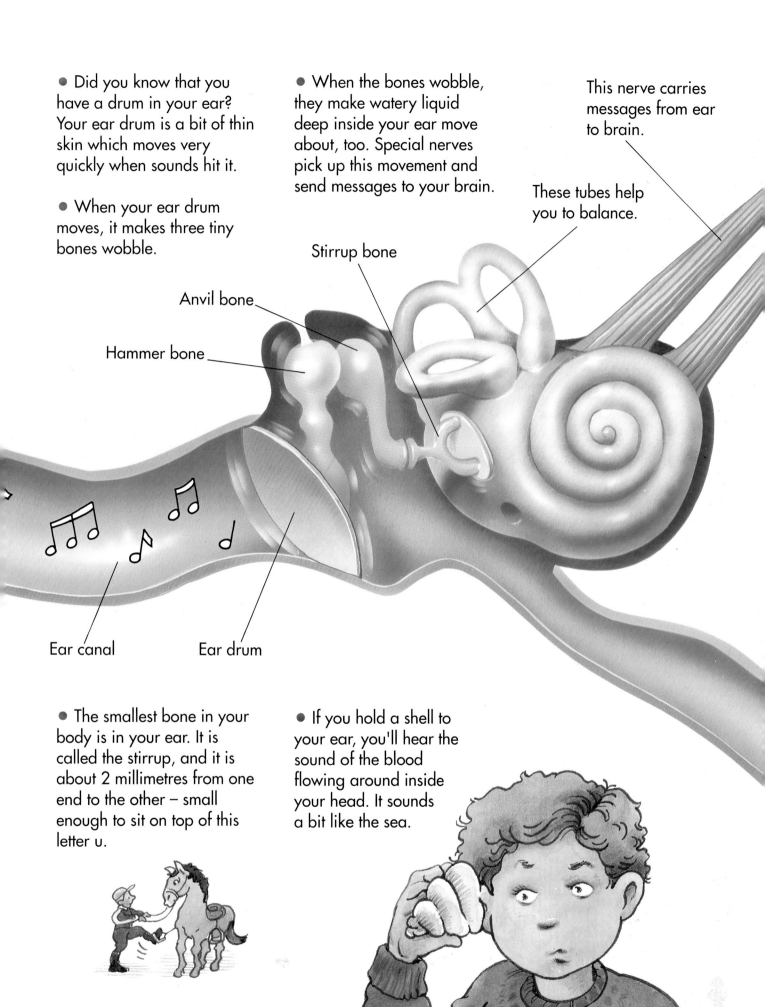

- Did you know that you have a drum in your ear? Your ear drum is a bit of thin skin which moves very quickly when sounds hit it.

- When your ear drum moves, it makes three tiny bones wobble.

- When the bones wobble, they make watery liquid deep inside your ear move about, too. Special nerves pick up this movement and send messages to your brain.

This nerve carries messages from ear to brain.

These tubes help you to balance.

Stirrup bone

Anvil bone

Hammer bone

Ear canal

Ear drum

- The smallest bone in your body is in your ear. It is called the stirrup, and it is about 2 millimetres from one end to the other – small enough to sit on top of this letter u.

- If you hold a shell to your ear, you'll hear the sound of the blood flowing around inside your head. It sounds a bit like the sea.

What is my nose for?

Your nose is for smelling things, and it also helps your tongue with tasting. It can do this because tiny bits of food are carried by air up into your nose when you eat.

• When a cold bungs your nose up, air can't get to the nose nerves and you can't taste your food properly.

The bits are far too small to see, but nerves inside your nose find them and send messages about them to your brain.

• Here's a way to see how much you taste things with your nose. You'll need someone to help you.

1 Get two different flavours of fruit yogurt.

2 Shut your eyes tight and hold your nose.

3 See if you can tell which yogurt you are eating.

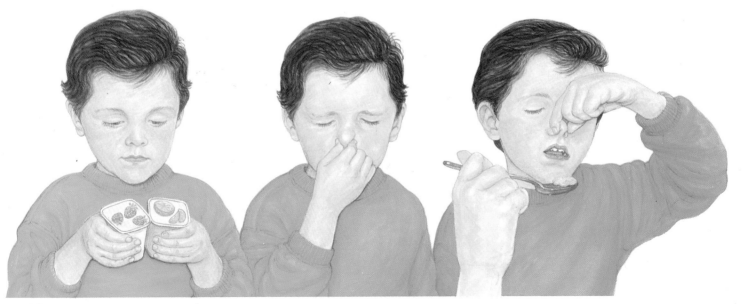

● To see how your tongue helps you to speak, put your finger on it and try to say 'Hello'.

What is my tongue for?

Your tongue is for tasting things, but it also helps you to speak and sing. It is covered with tiny little bumps called tastebuds, which send messages along nerves to your brain about all the delicious things you eat or drink.

Why do teeth fall out?

● When you are grown up, you will have between 28 and 32 teeth.

As you grow up, most parts of your body get bigger. But your teeth can't grow bigger, and so you have to change them.

When you are small, you have twenty small teeth called milk teeth. These start to fall out when you are five or six years old, to let new, bigger teeth grow in their place.

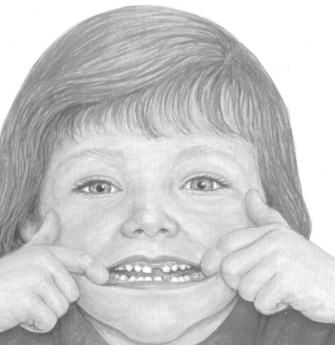

Why do I get ill sometimes?

When a part of your body stops working properly, you get ill. You don't feel right. Perhaps your tummy hurts, or you may have lots of itchy spots on your skin. Illness often happens because things called germs get inside your body.

● Sometimes your body has to fight and kill germs. The doctor may give you medicine to help it to do this.

● Some germs like dirt. Washing your body and cleaning your teeth help to keep these germs away.

TRANSPORT
AND
BUILDINGS

Which is the fastest car?

A British car called *Thrust 2* set the world land speed record in 1983. Using an aircraft jet engine in place of a normal car engine, it reached nearly 1020 kilometres an hour.

• The first car to go faster than 100 kilometres an hour was battery-powered. It was called *La Jamais Contente*, and it did this nearly 100 years ago, in 1899.

• The world's fastest sailing craft are sailboards. In good winds, they can zip across the water at more than 80 kilometres an hour.

Spirit of Australia

Which is the fastest boat?

Hydroplanes skim over the water almost as if flying. In 1977, Ken Warby roared to 556 kilometres an hour in his jet-powered *Spirit of Australia*.

Thrust 2

● To carry astronauts to the Moon in the 1960s and 1970s, the Saturn-Apollo rockets had to travel more than 40 times as fast as a jumbo jet. But the top speed of the astronauts' moon buggy was only 16 kilometres an hour!

SR-71A *Blackbird*

● One of the quickest ways to travel without an engine is on skis.

Which is the fastest plane?

The fastest aircraft are planes with jet engines. The world record was set back in 1976, when the USA's SR-71A reached an amazing 3530 kilometres an hour! It was nicknamed *Blackbird*.

Why do cars need petrol?

A car needs petrol for the same reason that you need food – to give it energy to move. It's hard to tell by looking at it, but petrol has lots of energy locked up inside it. This energy is set free inside a car engine, so it can be used to turn road wheels.

● Many toy cars use electrical energy, stored in batteries. There are a few ordinary cars that run on batteries, too.

● Petrol is made from oil, and it has energy because it comes from things that were once living! Oil formed millions of years ago, from the bodies of tiny plants and animals.

Exhaust pipe

Petrol tank

● Petrol is kept in a tank. It is pumped along a pipe to the engine.

Pistons

What happens inside car engines?

Petrol is mixed with air inside a car engine and then set on fire by an electric spark. This makes the air and petrol explode with a bang.

This explosion pushes engine parts called pistons up and down very quickly. The pistons make a rod called the crankshaft spin round. The crankshaft makes other rods spin, and they turn the road wheels.

Spark plug

Spark

Piston

Cylinder

Crankshaft

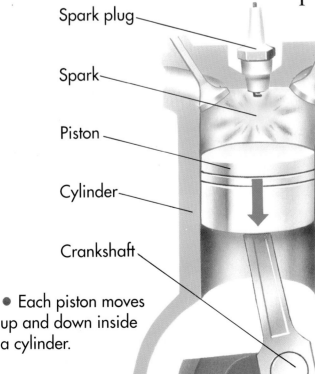

• Each piston moves up and down inside a cylinder.

Why don't ships sink?

When things are put into water they make room for themselves by pushing it aside. Although ships are heavy, they are hollow with high sides. This means they can settle quite low in the water, pushing a lot of it aside. In fact, a ship won't sink unless it is overloaded and becomes heavier than the water it pushes aside.

● You push water aside when you get into a bath. That's why you have to be careful not to overfill it!

How do submarines sink?

Submarines sink by making themselves too heavy to float. Water is let into special tanks to add weight. When it's time for the submarine to resurface, the water is pumped out.

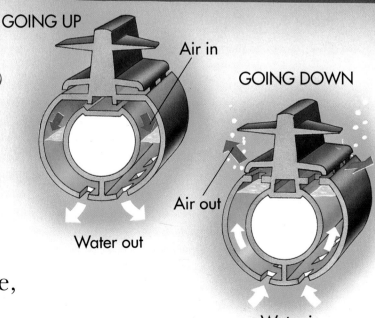

GOING UP

Air in

GOING DOWN

Air out

Water out

Water in

Which ships fly?

Although hovercraft travel across water, they don't float in it like ships. Instead, they hover just above the waves, held up by a cushion of air.

● Hovercraft can travel over land as well as water.

● This strange-looking diving suit was invented over 200 years ago. The tubes carried air to and from the surface.

● One of the earliest submarines was built by Dutchman Cornelius van Drebbel and tested in the 1620s. Twelve oarsmen rowed a wooden boat below the surface of the Thames River, in England.

What are houses made from?

Most houses are made from bricks, but they can be built out of almost anything – as long as it's strong and it keeps out the weather. Builders like to use materials they can get hold of easily – bricks or stone, wood, reeds, or mud.

● Bricklayers put mortar between the bricks. Mortar is a mixture of water, sand and cement, and it glues the bricks together.

● Houses protect us from the heat in summer, and the cold and rain in winter.

● There are about 12,000 bricks in the outside walls of a two-storey house.

● Some birds use mud to build their homes, but it's not shaped into little bricks!

● There aren't any bricks in the middle of a forest, but there's plenty of wood for building cabins.

● In the marshes of southern Iraq, in the Middle East, people use bundles of river reeds to build beautiful homes.

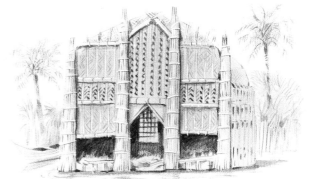

● In hot places such as Africa, people often build with mud and straw. The mixture dries hard in the sunshine.

Why do houses need holes?

Most houses start with holes in the ground. The holes are filled with runny concrete, which hardens as it sets. The rest of the house is then built on top of this firm base, called the foundations.

● Many diggers have a wide front bucket, as well as the digging bucket at the back.

● A digger can dig a trench as fast as 20 people with spades.

● The biggest earth-scooping buckets can hold five large family cars. They are on huge mining machines called excavators, which are about ten times bigger than the average digger.

● Diggers also dig holes for swimming pools, rubbish heaps and top-secret underground hiding places!

What do diggers do?

A digger does much more than dig. Its wide front bucket is brilliant at scooping rubble into a truck. A scissor-like bucket can also be fitted to the front, to grab and lift logs and pipes.

● A huge hammer can be fitted to a digger, allowing it to smash up rocks.

How are bridges built?

Like buildings, bridges start with deep foundation holes. These are filled with metal and concrete, then towers called piers are built on top. The deck is often made from sections, hoisted into place by cranes. Finally, the road or railway is laid on top of the deck.

● It takes a team of 29 painters three years to paint Scotland's 521-metre-long Forth Railway Bridge. When they finish, they have to start all over again!

● Deck sections are brought to the site on barges, towed by tugboats.

Deck

Pier

● Soldiers break step when crossing small bridges. If they all marched across in step together, the bridge might bounce. Too much bouncing, and it might break!

● If army ants have to cross gaps, some of them make a living bridge for the others to crawl over.

Do bridges sway about in the wind?

Bridges can bend and sway about as much as 2 or 3 metres – but don't worry, they're meant to! If bridges were completely stiff and rigid, a very strong wind might crack them.

Which bridge can break in two?

London's Tower Bridge carries traffic over the river Thames. The roadway is built in two halves, which can be raised or lowered like drawbridges. When a tall ship sails up the river, each half of the bridge lifts up so that the ship can pass through.

● Bungee-jumpers love the Royal Gorge Bridge in Colorado, USA. At 321 metres above the surface of the river, it's the highest bridge in the world.

● Tower Bridge isn't named for its tall towers, but after its neighbour, the Tower of London.

INVENTIONS

Why do people invent things?

Inventors try to solve problems. They think about people's needs, and come up with an answer. When an inventor noticed how inconvenient big umbrellas were, he invented a folding one that would fit in a bag.

Gone to buy some glue!

● Post-it notes were invented by accident when someone made a glue that didn't stick properly. You could stick down a piece of paper, peel it off, and then re-stick it!

● From the moment you wake up you're surrounded by inventions. Pillows, light bulbs, and even cornflakes all help to give us an easier, comfier life.

● Some inventions are just for fun. The first Frisbees were empty pie tins belonging to a baker called Joseph Frisbie. When some of his customers tossed the tins to each other in the park, the idea for the Frisbee was born.

● Safety pins
were introduced
almost 200 years ago,
but have a much longer
history. Their inventor copied
the idea from clasps worn by
the Ancient Egyptians.

Is everything invented?

No it isn't! An invention is something new like a paper-clip, which never existed before someone thought of it. But things like coal and rubber weren't invented. They were already in the world, and just had to be discovered.

● When people first discovered the milky juice of the rubber tree they used it to make rubber. Later, someone invented rubber tyres for cars and bicycles.

Where do inventors get their ideas?

Inventors get ideas for their inventions in lots of different places. Some of them study plants and animals to see how they have solved their problems. Others look at ideas from other places or from the past. Very few ideas come out of the blue.

● Burdock seeds are covered with tiny hooks that stick to things, but can be pulled off. An engineer who noticed this used his discovery to make Velcro for fastenings.

Why does my watch tick?

More than 20 tiny wheels are packed neatly inside your watch. You can hear them tick and tock as the teeth of one wheel lock into the teeth of the next. The moving wheels keep time, and slowly turn the hands around the watch face.

How did people manage before clocks?

Before clocks were invented, people judged the time by looking at the Sun. They got up at sunrise, and went to bed when it was dark. They ate lunch when the Sun was up above, and ate dinner when it set in the west.

● Sailors usually work for four hours at a time. Bells ring every half an hour – one after half an hour, two after an hour and so on. When eight bells sound, the shift is over, and the sailors can take a well-earned rest.

How does a grandfather keep good time?

A tall grandfather clock has a long pendulum that swings back and forth in a steady rhythm. With every swing, wheels inside the clock slowly turn, moving the hands round the face. Winding the clock with a key stops it slowing down.

● Sundials are one of the oldest kinds of clock. Instead of a moving hand, they have a shadow, cast by the Sun. As the Earth turns during the day, the 'hand' moves around the clock.

What were the first cars like?

The first cars were steam engines on wheels – noisy, smoky machines that scared other road-users! But these steam cars soon got quicker and easier to drive. They were used for nearly 30 years, until they were replaced by faster cars with petrol engines.

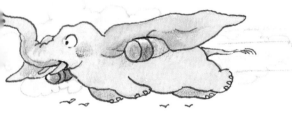

● In the 1930s, planes carried 20 passengers at the most. By the 1970s, the new jumbo jets could seat up to 500! Soon, new super-jumbos will carry as many as 850 people!

How do you ride on air?

People ride on air every time they travel on a hovercraft. The hovercraft was invented by Christopher Cockerell in 1959. He discovered that trapping a cushion of air beneath a boat lifts it up above the waves, allowing it to travel much faster.

• The penny-farthing bicycle was invented in the 1860s. It had two wheels – one very large and one very small – and was named after two British coins of the time – the large penny and the tiny farthing.

• Eveyone knows about seat belts for people to wear, but did you know that cats and dogs can wear them too? So clunk-click, Rover/Felix!

• The first cars weren't allowed to go faster than 3 km/h. And someone had to walk in front with a flag to warn other road-users!

Which bikes have sails?

The fastest superbikes have solid wheels and flat frames that work in the same way as a sail. As the bike zooms along, its wheels and frame catch the wind, which helps to push the bike forward – just as it does on a boat. But most of the power still comes from turning the pedals!

How can you fit 1,000 books in your pocket?

There's room for about 1,000 storybooks on a CD-ROM – a small compact disc that's as thin as your fingernail and can fit in a pocket. Words, pictures and sounds can all be stored on CD-ROMs, but they only work with a computer, so you can't read one on the bus – yet!

● The Egyptians were one of the first peoples to write with ink. They made it by mixing black soot with sticky tree sap.

● Just like dinosaurs, the typewriter will soon be extinct. It was a new invention in 1873, but has now been replaced by computers and word-processors.

● Felt-tip pens went on sale in Japan in 1962. Their inventor hoped that the pen's soft tip would make people's handwriting more graceful – like the brushstrokes in Japanese calligraphy.

● Today's pocket calculators can carry out calculations much quicker than you can move your fingers. They are as powerful as the huge computers of the 1960s.

Which computer was as big as a bus?

The first computer was about as long as four buses and was called Colossus. It was built in Britain and was switched on in 1943. Very few people knew about it at the time, because one of its first jobs was to crack secret codes in the war.

Who was Mr Biro?

Ladislao Biro invented the ballpoint pen in 1938. It contained a tube of long-lasting, quick-drying ink, which rolled evenly onto the paper thanks to a tiny ball at the tip. Although Biro called his pen a ballpoint, most people now call their ballpoint a biro!

Why does the telephone ring?

The telephone rings to let you know that someone wants to speak to you! So if your friend dials your number, your phone rings out. When you answer, an electric current carries your voice along the line and your friend hears you loud and clear!

● Today, most telephone exchanges connect calls automatically with computers.

● Telephone calls used to be connected by hand. An operator asked which telephone number you wanted and plugged in the correct wire.

How can glass link the world?

• Telephones come in all shapes and sizes, from tiny mobiles to cartoon characters. But they all have two main parts – the transmitter you talk into and the receiver which you listen to.

Optical fibres are hair-thin strands of glass, twisted into cable. They have been laid under all the oceans and act as highways for anything from phone calls to TV programmes. Information travels along them at the speed of light.

Are phone lines just for voices?

Voices aren't the only things that travel along a phone line. With a videophone, you can see a picture of who's telephoning as well. With a fax, you can send letters, photos and drawings. And computers use phone lines to communicate with one another too!

• There are over 100 million telephones in the United States. In Washington DC, there are more phones than people!

How can you fight a hungry dinosaur?

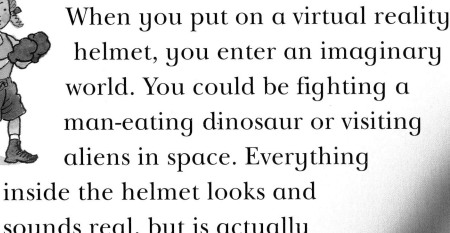

When you put on a virtual reality helmet, you enter an imaginary world. You could be fighting a man-eating dinosaur or visiting aliens in space. Everything inside the helmet looks and sounds real, but is actually created by a computer.

● As you press buttons in the special data-glove, the computer changes the pictures you see and the sounds you hear.

● Anyone can be an inventor! What would you like to invent?

HISTORY

How many dinosaurs were there?

There were lots of different dinosaurs. Scientists have already named about 300 kinds, and new ones are being found all the time. Some dinosaurs were big, others were tiny. Some were fierce meat-eaters, others were gentle vegetarians which browsed on plants.

Apatosaurus (plants)

Spinosaurus (meat)

Iguanodon (plants)

Styracosaurus (plants)   Panoplosaurus (plants)   Oviraptor (meat)   Stygimoloch (plants)

● Dinosaurs were reptiles. Today's reptiles include lizards, crocodiles, tortoises and snakes.

● Like most other reptiles, dinosaurs lived on land and had dry scaly skin. Their eggs had leathery shells, unlike birds' eggs which are hard and brittle.

How long ago did dinosaurs live?

Dinosaurs lived MILLIONS and MILLIONS of years ago. The first ones appeared about 230 million years ago, and the last ones we know about died out over 65 million years ago. Compared to this, human history is just a hiccup – we've only been around for the last 2 million years.

● Dinosaurs ruled the Earth for a mind-boggling 165 million years!

Kentrosaurus (plants)

What happened to the dinosaurs?

Something very strange happened 65 million years ago. All the dinosaurs vanished, together with all the flying reptiles and most of the sea reptiles. No one knows for sure what happened to them.

● Many scientists think giant rocks from outer space smashed into the Earth, throwing up great clouds of dust which blotted out the Sun. This changed the weather and killed off most plants. First the plant-eating dinosaurs died of cold and hunger, then the meat-eaters.

● Perhaps the dinosaurs were poisoned by new kinds of plants.

● A few people believe that sea reptiles like Elasmosaurus didn't die out, and that families of them now live in big lakes like Scotland's Loch Ness!

● Archaeopteryx looked like a dinosaur with feathers, but it wasn't. It lived 140 million years ago, and it is the oldest bird we know about. It was a very strange bird, though, because it had a tail, clawed fingers and teeth, just like a dinosaur.

Are there any dinosaurs around today?

Although there aren't any true dinosaurs alive today, we do have some of their relatives. Scientists think that birds developed from dinosaurs, because their skeletons are so similar. So look carefully the next time you see a bird nesting in a tree or hopping across the grass!

Why do we call Egyptians ancient?

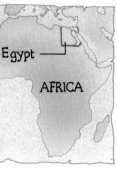

Egypt — AFRICA

We call the Egyptians ancient because they lived such a long time ago – not because they all reached a ripe old age! The first Egyptians were farmers about 8,000 years ago. Within a few thousand years, Egypt had become one of the most powerful countries in the world.

● Will people be studying us in 5,000 years' time? What will they think about the way we live now?

● The Egyptians usually built tombs for dead kings on the river's western bank, where the Sun sets. They believed that their kings went to meet the Sun god when they died.

● Egypt is mostly sandy desert, where nothing grows. The Ancient Egyptians settled on the banks of the river Nile, where there was plenty of water for themselves and their crops.

● The Ancient Egyptians didn't know about distant parts of the world. But they did explore parts of Asia and Africa. And their merchants bought wood, gold, ivory, spices and even apes from nearby countries.

Why were the Egyptians great?

The Egyptians were so good at farming that they became very rich. They built fantastic temples for their gods, and huge pointed tombs called pyramids where they buried their kings. They had armies and ships and courts of law. Their priests studied the stars and their craftspeople made beautiful things from gold and silver.

Mediterranean Sea

Giza
Memphis
Saqqara

LOWER EGYPT

Red Sea

UPPER EGYPT

Abydos

Valley of the Kings
Thebes

Nile River

Farming land
Desert

Who were the Ancient Greeks?

The Ancient Greeks were people who lived in Greece from around 3,500 years ago. But they didn't live only in Greece. Some lived to the north and the east, in lands that we now call Bulgaria and Turkey. Others lived on small rocky islands in the Aegean Sea.

● Many Greek people set sail for North Africa, Turkey, Italy and France. They found safe harbours, where they built new homes and towns, and cleared the land for farming.

Greek homeland
Greek colonies

FRANCE

ITALY

Mediterranean Sea

NORTH AFRICA

Aegean Sea

TURKEY

● By 500BC the Greek world was large, rich and powerful. It stretched from France in the west to Turkey in the east.

● Wherever they went, the Greek settlers took their own way of life. They must have looked odd to the locals!

● The Greeks were a talented people. They had good laws and strong armies. They built beautiful temples and theatres. And they were great thinkers, artists and athletes.

Why did Greece grow bigger and bigger?

Greece and its homelands were small, and much of its land was too rocky for farming. By about 750BC, there was little room left for new towns or farms, and food began to run short. Because of this, many people left Greece to look for new places to live, and the Greek world began to grow.

Who were the Romans?

The Romans were people who came from Rome. About 2,000 years ago they became so powerful that they began to conquer the lands around them. By AD100 they ruled a huge empire, and were one of the mightiest peoples in the ancient world.

- Different parts of the empire had very different climates. Romans boiled in Egypt, where the summers were sweltering...

BRITAIN
Hadrian's Wall
London
FRANCE (Gaul)
•Lyon
Alps
SPAIN
Pyrenees
ITALY
•Rome
Pompeii •
Carthage
AFRICA

- An old legend says that the city of Rome was first started by a man called Romulus. He and his twin brother Remus had been abandoned by their parents and looked after by a wolf!

Did all the Romans live in Rome?

● ...but they shivered in the icy Swiss Alps and in northern Britain. These were the coldest places in the whole empire.

The city of Rome wasn't big enough for all the Romans! All in all, there were about 50 million people in the empire, which stretched from Britain in the north to Africa in the south. Everyone in the empire was protected by Rome's armies, but had to obey Rome's laws.

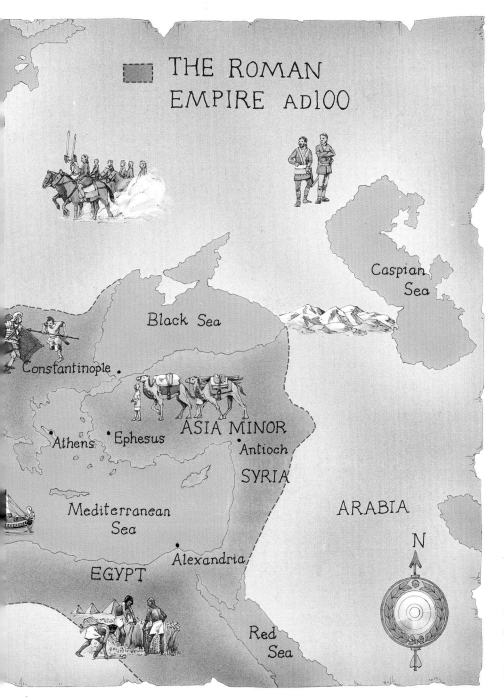

THE ROMAN EMPIRE AD100

Caspian Sea

Black Sea

Constantinople

Athens • Ephesus ASIA MINOR
• Antioch

SYRIA

Mediterranean Sea

ARABIA

N

Alexandria

EGYPT

Red Sea

3,000 miles

● It would have taken nearly 100 days to ride from one end of the empire to the other. It was a journey of over 3,000 Roman miles, about 5,000 kilometres.

Where can you visit a Roman town?

Pompeii was a bustling town not far from Rome. In the year AD 79, a nearby volcano erupted, and buried the town in ash. Pompeii lay hidden for centuries until, one day, some farmers discovered its Roman remains. Today you can visit to see what life was like in Roman times.

● Archaeologists have studied Pompeii since the 1800s, and have uncovered an almost-perfect Roman town.

MAKING MODELS

1 People were buried by the volcano's ash. Over the years, their bodies rotted away, leaving people-shaped holes in the hardened ash, or rock.

2 Archaeologists used the holes as moulds. They poured plaster inside, and waited for it to set.

3 Chipping away at the rock left plaster models of the Romans. Archaeologists study these carefully to learn about Roman life.

● Mount Vesuvius was an active volcano. As it erupted, showers of ash poured onto Pompeii, killing the people with poisonous fumes.

● The Roman empire grew weaker and weaker. It was attacked by warriors from the north and the east, who split up the empire into many small kingdoms.

How do we know about the Romans?

The Roman empire came to an end in the 470s. Yet Roman buildings, mosaics, writings, paintings and weapons have all survived. Remains like these tell us about the people and the way they lived.

● Some Roman finds are rather peculiar. Archaeologists in London have dug up a pair of black leather knickers. Who could have lost them all those years ago?

What were the Middle Ages in the middle of?

We call the years between the ancient world and the modern world in Europe the Middle Ages. They started in the 470s, when rule by the Romans came to an end, and they finished in the 1450s.

NORTH AMERICA

IROQUOIS

Newfoundland

ANASAZI

Pueblo Bonito

ATLANTIC OCEAN

MAYA

AZTECS

SOUTH AMERICA

INCAS

PACIFIC OCEAN

● The Romans once ruled most of Europe and North Africa. Then fierce warriors invaded, splitting Roman lands into many small kingdoms. By the 1450s Europe had larger countries again, more like those of today.

● The map above includes the people and places talked about in this book.

● In the Middle Ages, no one knew what the whole world looked like.

VIKINGS

ASIA

EUROPE

Venice

MONGOLS

JAPAN

PERSIA

CHINA

Leshan

Mediterranean
Sea

INDIA

Angkor
Wat

Fez

ARABIA

Timbuktu

AFRICA

Ife

Great
Zimbabwe

INDIAN
OCEAN

AUSTRALIA

NEW ZEALAND

MAORIS

● This is what Arab map-makers thought the world looked like in the 1150s. It shows Asia, North Africa and Europe. Neither the Arabs nor the Europeans knew about other parts of the world.

● Most people thought the world was flat. Sailors were afraid of falling over the edge if they went on long voyages!

Why did castles have moats?

Moats were deep wide ditches filled with water, which made it harder for enemies to break into a castle. Friendly visitors could cross the moat over a drawbridge. But when enemies attacked, the drawbridge was raised.

● Spies and traitors were chained up in the castle's dungeons. These were dark and damp and full of rats and spiders!

● One way to beat enemies who shut themselves up in a castle was to surround it – and wait! This was called a siege. When the castle ran out of food and water, the people inside had to give in.

● Strong stone walls were built to protect towns and cities all over the world. The picture on the right shows Great Zimbabwe, a walled city begun in the 1000s by the Shona people of southern Africa.

● Pueblo Bonito was one of the walled towns built by the Anasazi people of North America between 950 and 1300.

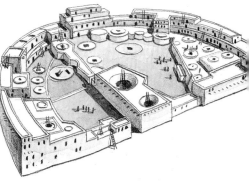

● In the 1300s, people in Europe learned how to make big guns called cannons. In time it became easier to blow up castles – if the guns went off properly!

Who made a new home in the New World?

In 1620, English settlers sailed to America on the *Mayflower*. These settlers are sometimes called the Pilgrim Fathers, but there were actually whole families on the ship! The Pilgrims wanted to start a new life in America and they became the first colonists in New England.

- Every year, we remember the Pilgrims' first harvest when we celebrate Thanksgiving Day.

- Winters were hard and the Pilgrims' crops failed, but nearby tribes showed them how to grow new crops like corn and potatoes.

- The Pilgrims left England because they weren't happy with the king. They weren't the only ones! In 1605 there'd been a plot to blow him up when he opened Parliament—the Gunpowder Plot.

Who built the best home for the next world?

The Taj Mahal is a magnificent tomb in India. The Mogul ruler Shah Jahan built it for his favorite wife, who died in 1629. It was made of white marble and took 21 years to build. The outside is decorated with flowers and passages from the Muslim holy book, *The Koran*.

- The explorer Christopher Columbus discovered America in 1492. No one had ever sailed so far west. Some people thought he might fall off the edge of the world!

Who was the 'last' king of France?

Louis XVI was a French king. He and his queen lived extravagantly – and paid for it by taxing his people. They got fed up of being poor and decided not to have a king anymore. They set up a parliament so they ruled themselves. There were a couple more kings later, but the people soon got fed up with the idea again.

● Queen Marie Antoinette of France was spoilt and rich. When she was told there was no bread for the starving peasants, she couldn't see why they didn't eat cake instead!

● Louis XVI and his queen both had their heads chopped off, by a new machine called the guillotine.

● The final straw for the French was the 'gabelle'. This new tax made salt too dear for most people. And in the days before fridges, salt was about the only way to keep meat fresh.

● President Washington's head can still be seen on coins and bills today.

● The United States had to fight to become free, or independent, of Britain. The war was called the Revolutionary War.

Who was the first president of the United States?

George Washington became the first president of the United States in 1789. Before then, the British king had ruled America—from nearly 3,000 miles across the ocean.

● The American people were fed up with paying taxes to the British king. One night a few of them ransacked a British tea ship in Boston harbor and threw all the tea chests overboard. We call it the Boston Tea Party—some party!

Who steamed into the twentieth century?

Many of today's machines were invented in the 1800s. Factories were built and people grew richer. It was cheaper and quicker to make things, such as clothes. Today we call this time the Industrial Revolution, because there were so many changes in industry.

● Inventions like the new steam trains changed everyone's lives. It meant more people could afford to travel.

● The Great Exhibition of 1851 in London showed off all the new goods that were being made. Even the building was amazing —the Crystal Palace was built entirely of glass and iron.

● All this industry needed power, which came from coal. Even children worked in the coal mines—because they were small they could get into the tiniest tunnels.

● Families were a lot bigger in the 1800s than they are today. Many families had ten children or even more!

COUNTRIES AND PEOPLES

What is a country?

A country is an independent land with its own government. The government runs the country, and makes laws which the people must keep. A country has its own name, and its borders are normally agreed by other countries around the world.

● Each country has its own money, called its currency, with its own style of coins and bank-notes. There are roubles in Russia and francs in France.

● All countries have their own stamps, which often carry a picture of the country's ruler. Some stamps show a country's wildlife, or mark an important discovery.

● People wave their national flags at parades, sports events and celebrations.

CHINA

BRAZIL

SWEDEN

GREECE

GERMANY

ISRAEL

Why do countries fly flags?

Every country has its own flag, which is a sort of national badge. Each flag is different. Its design may include coloured stripes, star and sun patterns, or religious signs such as crosses or crescents. Flags are flown on special occasions, as a symbol of a country and its people.

● Every country has its own special song called a national anthem. It is sung to show respect for a country and its history.

SUDAN

AUSTRALIA

UNITED KINGDOM

CANADA

TURKEY

ARGENTINA

SOUTH KOREA

JAMAICA

AUSTRIA

Which country has the most people?

Well over a billion people live in China, and about 48,000 new babies are born there every day. You'd think that meant a lot of birthdays, but in China everyone celebrates their birthday at the same time – the Chinese New Year!

- Chinese New Year is celebrated by Chinese people all over the world in late January or early February. There are spectacular street processions.

HAPPY BIRTHDAY

- The world's biggest-ever birthday party was on July 4, 1991. It celebrated the birthday not of a person but of two countries – the USA and Canada. Over 75,000 people turned up!

Which is the biggest country?

Russia is so big that it takes eight days to cross it by train! As children set off for school in the city of Moscow in the west, others are already going home in the eastern port of Vladivostok.

MOSCOW

VLADIVOSTOK

Where is there land, but no countries?

The vast frozen land around the South Pole is called Antarctica. It is not a country – it has no people, no government and no flag. Many countries have signed an agreement, promising to keep Antarctica as a wilderness for scientists to study.

● Nobody lives in Antarctica except for a few hundred scientists, who go there to study rocks, the weather, and the plant and animal life.

Where are there only two seasons?

Many tropical countries have only two seasons in the year. One is very wet, and the other very dry. Not many trees manage to survive the dry months, and animals travel hundreds of kilometres searching for food and water.

● Many animals migrate in different seasons. Every year, swarms of monarch butterflies leave Mexico and fly 3,000 kilometres to spend the summer by cool Canadian lakes.

● During the dry season, the ground is baked hard by the hot Sun. Clouds of dust cover everything and everyone.

● In the dry season, herds of wildebeest and zebra cross the grasslands of central Africa. They follow the thunderclouds in search of rainwater and fresh grass.

EQUATOR

● Tropical lands lie near the equator. They are the warmest parts of the Earth.

Where does it pour for a month?

Some parts of India and Southeast Asia have long heavy downpours called monsoons. Big black clouds are blown in from the sea during the summer months. Once the rain starts, it can last for weeks, flooding the fields and the streets.

Who rides on a snowmobile?

• A dog team can pull a sled about 80 kilometres in a day. A snowmobile covers that in an hour!

Many of the people who live in icy Alaska and northern Canada travel across the frozen snow on powerful sleds called snowmobiles. Not long ago, sleds were pulled by husky dogs, but nowadays these are only raced for fun.

• Trains in Tokyo, Japan, are so crowded that railway staff called crushers have to push in the passengers while the doors close.

• Fishermen in Portugal paint 'magic' eyes on their boats to watch over them at sea and bring them safely to harbour.

Where do you park your bike in China?

There are millions and millions of people in China, and millions and millions of bikes! So all Chinese cities have huge cycle parks, where an attendant gives your bike a number, and helps you to find it again later.

Who paints pictures on trucks?

The truck drivers of Afghanistan are very proud of their trucks. They paint holy pictures all over them, covering every last centimetre in bright, colourful patterns. Even the wheel nuts are painted different colours.

● The Afghans may drape their trucks with silver chains, and even stick on ring-pulls from drink cans as decorations.

127

Who writes with a paintbrush?

In China and Japan, handwriting can be an art. Instead of dashing something off with a pen, people sometimes paint words slowly and beautifully with a brush and ink. Artists often frame their work, and hang it on the wall just like a picture.

● The art of beautiful handwriting is called calligraphy. Japanese children learn calligraphy at school.

● About 50,000 different symbols may be used to write Chinese. Luckily, school children only have to learn about 5,000 of them.

Who reads back-to-front?

To read a book in Arabic or Hebrew, you have to work from right to left. So if this book were in Arabic, the first page would be where the index is now.

Which country speaks over 800 languages?

Papua New Guinea is a land of many languages. Most of the people live in small villages, deep in the rainforest or high up in the misty mountains. Some are so cut off from each other that their languages are quite different.

● In many areas of Papua New Guinea, people can only talk to each other through a translator.

● Around 5,000 languages are spoken around the world. Here are just a few ways to say "hello".

Jambo!

Namaste!

¡Hola!

Czesc!

Dag!

Swahili   Hindi   Spanish   Polish   Dutch

● There's a place in New Zealand with 85 letters in its name. And there's another in France with just one!

Y

Taumatawhakatangihangakoauauotamateaturipukakapikimaungahoronukupokaiwhenuakitanatahu

Where are wheatfields bigger than countries?

The rolling grasslands of Canada and the USA are planted with wheat as far as the eye can see. One Canadian wheatfield was so big, it was double the size of the European country, San Marino!

● Huge combine harvesters have to work in teams to harvest the gigantic wheatfields.

● More people eat rice than wheat. Rice plants need to stand in water, and are grown on flooded land called paddy fields.

Where does chocolate grow on trees?

Chocolate is made from the seeds of the cacao tree. Sadly, the trees don't grow everywhere – just in the hot, wet parts of South America, southeast Asia and West Africa.

Which country has more sheep than people?

● In Thailand, coconut farmers train monkeys to harvest their crop. The monkeys scamper up the trunks of the palm trees and throw down the fruits.

Although there are more than 17 million people in Australia, most live around the coast. In the centre people run enormous sheep farms. At the last count, there were 147 million sheep – nearly nine times the number of people!

Who lights the lamps at New Year?

The Hindu New Year is called the Festival of Light – and no wonder! Towns are strung with lights, and lamps shine from every door and window. The women make beautiful floor pictures with coloured chalks, flour and sand, and decorate them with glowing candles.

● Chinese New Year celebrations can last up to 15 days. They begin between the middle of January and the middle of February.

Who brings in the New Year with a bang?

New Year in China starts with beating drums, crashing cymbals, fireworks and a lion or dragon dancing through the streets. All this noise is meant to chase away the bad days of the past and bring luck in the future.

● The Hindus call their New Year festival Diwali. Diwali falls not in January, but in October or November.

● On New Year's Eve in Ecuador in South America, people burn the Old Year on a bonfire! It's a figure they make from bits of straw.

Who blows a horn at New Year?

The Jewish New Year festival of Rosh Hashanah begins with the blowing of a curly ram's horn. The sound calls people to the synagogue to pray for God's forgiveness for the things they've done wrong in the past year. As the new year begins they can make a fresh start.

● Rosh Hashanah falls in October or November. People eat apples and bread dipped in honey in the hope of a sweet year to come!

Where do elephants glow in the dark?

For the Sri Lankan festival of the Esala Perahera, elephants are decorated with beautiful hangings and strings of electric lights. More than 50 elephants take part in a night-time procession, along with thousands of drummers and dancers, who crack whips and wave colourful banners.

● The leprechaun of Irish folktales is a little green man. The green shamrock is Ireland's national flower.

When do people eat green food?

Saint Patrick is the patron saint of Ireland, and green is the country's national colour. Saint Patrick's Day falls on March 17th, and for Irish people everywhere it's a time of wild celebration. Some people even dye party food and drink green!

When is the Day of the Dead?

The Day of the Dead is a Mexican holiday which takes place every year on November 2nd, All Soul's Day. People remember dead friends and relatives by taking flowers and candles to their graves, and having picnics there.

● Brightly painted papier-mâché skeletons are made for the Day of the Dead celebrations.

● February is carnival time in many countries, with glittering parades and music.

● The Esala Perahera procession takes place in Kandy, Sri Lanka, at the time of the July full moon.

Could people live in space?

They already have! Some astronauts have lived in space stations spinning around the Earth for as long as a year. There are plans for much bigger stations, where people could live for 10 years, and even for settlements on Mars.

● It would take 8 months to reach Mars in a spacecraft. The crew would have to take everything they needed with them – the food for just one person would make a pile twice as big as a family car.

● There are plans for a huge wheel-shaped space station, measuring over 1 kilometre across.

● People have even lived under the sea, but not for longer than a few weeks at a time. They were working in underwater laboratories.

ANIMALS

● Female Queen Alexandra's birdwings are the world's biggest butterflies. Their wings are almost as big as this page!

● The blue whale is so long that eight elephants could stand along its back.

Giraffe
5.5 metres tall

Elephant
3.5 metres tall
7 tonnes

Ostrich
2.5 metres tall

● The giraffe is the tallest land animal. With its long neck, it can reach as high as a two-storey house.

● The mighty African elephant is almost three times as tall as you are. It can weigh as much as seven cars.

● The ostrich is the world's tallest and heaviest bird. It's as tall as a single-decker bus!

Which is the biggest animal?

The biggest animal that has ever lived is the blue whale – it is even larger than the biggest dinosaurs were. Blue whales can weigh as much as 150 cars!

Blue whale
30 metres long
150 tonnes

● The whale shark weighs as much as 40 cars. It's the world's biggest fish.

People
1.6 to 1.9 metres tall

Whale shark
15 metres long
40 tonnes

● The reticulated python can grow to be as long as a row of six bicycles! It's the world's longest snake.

Reticulated python 10 metres long

What's the difference between sharks and dolphins?

Although sharks and dolphins look alike, they belong to two very different animal groups. Sharks are a kind of fish, but dolphins are members of another group, the mammals.

● You don't look anything like a dolphin, but you are a mammal, too!

● If an animal breathes air through lungs, and its babies feed on their mother's milk, it's a mammal. Most mammals have some fur or hair on their bodies.

Lungs

● If an animal has feathers and hatches out of a hard-shelled egg, it's a bird. All birds have wings, and most of them can fly.

● If an animal has six legs and three parts to its body, it's an insect. There are more kinds of insect in the world than all the other kinds of animal put together.

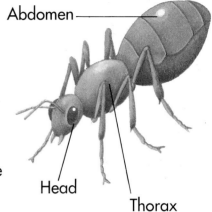

Abdomen

Head

Thorax

● If an animal has damp slimy skin, and is born in water but lives much of its life on land, it's an amphibian. Baby amphibians hatch out of jelly-like eggs.

● If an animal has a dry scaly skin and is born on land, it's a reptile. Most reptiles lay eggs with leathery skins.

● If an animal lives in water, breathing through gills and using fins to move, it's a fish. Most fish lay jelly-like eggs which hatch into baby fish.

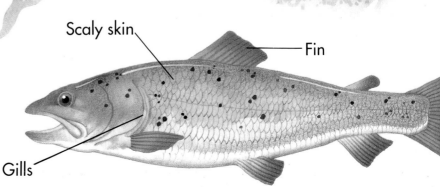

Scaly skin

Fin

Gills

141

What's the difference between frogs and toads?

Frogs usually have smooth skin and long legs for leaping. Most toads have lumpy skin and move their short thick bodies about by crawling.

Toad

Frog

...and alligators and crocodiles?

Crocodiles have longer, more pointed snouts than alligators. Crocodiles also have one very large tooth sticking up on each side when they close their mouths.

● Frogs and toads are both amphibians.

● Alligators and crocodiles are reptiles.

Crocodile

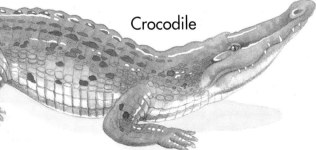

Alligator

...and between monkeys and apes?

The big difference between these animals is that monkeys have long tails, but apes don't have tails at all. There are lots of different kinds of monkey, but the only apes are gorillas, orang-utans, chimpanzees and gibbons.

Spider monkey

Orang-utan (ape)

● Monkeys and apes are mammals

● A woodlouse looks like it's an insect, but it isn't – it has too many legs! This creepy-crawly is related to crabs and lobsters.

● Rabbits and hares are both mammals.

...and rabbits and hares?

Hares have longer legs and ears than rabbits. Their whiskers are longer, too.

Why do animals have skeletons inside their bodies?

Not all animals have skeletons, but most large ones do. This is because the bigger an animal is, the more it needs a strong sturdy framework to hold its body together and carry its weight. Skeletons also protect soft inside parts, like brains and hearts.

Backbone ———

• Animals without backbones are called invertebrates. Insects, spiders, snails, worms, jellyfish, prawns and crabs are all invertebrates.

• Animals with backbones are called vertebrates. Fish are vertebrates, and so are amphibians, reptiles, birds and mammals.

Backbone

● Most animals' skeletons are made of bone, but a shark's skeleton is made of gristle. This isn't as hard as bone, but it's still tough. You have some at your nose tip.

● Insects, spiders, scorpions, centipedes and millipedes all have tough exoskeletons.

Millipede

● Lobsters, crabs and some beetles have really tough exoskeletons that work like armour, to protect them from attack.

● Squid are the biggest kind of invertebrate. The longest one ever found measured more than 17 metres from its head to the tip of its tentacles – longer than eight scuba divers!

Which animals have skeletons on the outside?

Most smaller animals have tough skins called exoskeletons. These outside skeletons do the same job as inside ones. They protect and support the animals' soft bodies.

● To grow larger, an animal has to break out of its old exoskeleton and grow a new one.

Do reptiles have skin like ours?

A reptile's skin is quite tough and horny, more like our fingernails than our skin. On snakes and lizards, most of the skin is covered with small scales that overlap one another. But crocodiles and turtles have an even tougher skin, with hard plates rather than scales.

● Snakes don't feel slimy. They're dry, cool and pleasant to touch.

● A reptile's scaly skin holds in water, and stops the animal from drying out. This is useful if you live in the desert, as many lizards do.

● A snake's old skin begins to split at the lips. The snake wriggles out head first, turning the skin inside out as it goes. The skin often comes off in one piece, in a perfect snake shape.

Why do snakes shed their skin?

Like your old clothes, a snake's skin wears out and needs replacing – often in a bigger size. So from three to seven times a year, the old skin splits open and peels off, and – hey presto! – there's a brand-new skin waiting underneath.

● In times of danger, the armadillo lizard turns into an armoured ball. It rolls on its back, grips its tail in its mouth and hides its soft belly behind a wall of scales and spines.

Why do some lizards have horns and spikes?

Horns and spikes are a good way of protecting an animal. Like a strong suit of armour, they make a lizard look fierce – and they also make a prickly mouthful for any animal that tries to attack.

Why do birds have feathers?

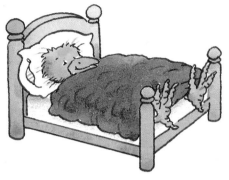

Feathers keep birds warm. They also help them to fly, by giving their wings and bodies a special sleek shape.

Each kind of bird has feathers of a different colour and pattern. Males are often brighter than females – their good looks help them to attract a mate!

● Birds' fluffy down feathers trap warm air next to their skin – in much the same way as a duvet keeps you warm in bed.

● Hummingbirds are among the world's smallest birds. The bee hummingbird lays its eggs in a nest the size of a walnut.

Which bird can fly backwards?

Hummingbirds are the helicopters of the bird world. They can fly in all directions – backwards, forwards, sideways, up and down. They can even hover on one spot.

• Birds can fly by flapping their wings up and down, or by gliding on still, outstretched wings.

Why can't penguins fly?

Penguins can't fly because their wings are too small to keep their heavy bodies up in the air. But penguins are very good swimmers and divers. They use their wings as paddles in the water.

• Most birds can fold their wings up close to their bodies. But penguins can't. They always hold their wings stiffly out to the side.

• Ostriches are too big to fly, but they can run at twice the speed of the fastest Olympic runners.

What is an insect?

An insect has three pairs of legs (that's six altogether), and three parts to its body. The first part is the head, the second is the thorax, and the third is the abdomen.

● Woodlice aren't insects. They belong to the same family as crabs, lobsters and shrimps. They don't get together very often though, as woodlice live on land, not in water.

● Like all insects, this hoverfly has three pairs of legs and three parts to its body.

Feeler

Head

Eye

Thorax

Mouth

Leg

When is a fly not a fly?

A true fly, such as a housefly, has only one pair of wings. Butterflies, dragonflies, damselflies, and mayflies all have two pairs of wings. So they're not really flies at all!

Wing

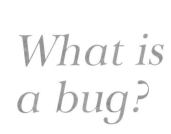

What is a bug?

Bugs are insects that have needle-like beaks. A bug uses its beak to cut open its food. Then it sucks up the tasty juices inside, using its beak like a straw.

● Bedbugs are the draculas of the insect world. At night, they look for sleeping humans to bite. Then they suck up the tasty blood!

● Centipedes have too many legs to be insects. One kind has 176 pairs!

Abdomen

● There are over a million kinds of insect – more than any other kind of animal in the world. And scientists are still finding new ones!

Are spiders insects?

No – a spider has eight legs, not six. What's more, its body has two parts instead of three. This is because the head and thorax are joined on a spider's body.

Why do caterpillars change into butterflies?

Every butterfly has to go through four different stages of its life before it is a fully grown adult. At each stage, it changes its size, its shape and its colour.

● Many kinds of insect change shape as they grow. This way of growing is called metamorphosis.

1 A butterfly lays its eggs on a plant the baby caterpillars eat.

2 The caterpillars eat hungrily, and grow very quickly.

● The babies that hatch from an insect's eggs are known as larvae – but many people just call them grubs.

● Caterpillars grow so quickly that their skin pops open. Underneath, there's brand new skin with plenty of growing room.

3 Each caterpillar makes itself a hard case called a pupa. Inside, its body turns into a kind of mushy soup.

● The pupa is like a strongbox. It keeps the insect's body safe while it changes shape.

NO ENTRY
REBUILDING
WORK
IN PROGRESS

152

● Not all insects change completely as they grow. A grasshopper's eggs hatch out into tiny nymphs, which look almost like their parents.

● Nymphs split their skins as they grow, but they don't make a pupa. They just slowly change into adults.

● A female butterfly lays as many as 50,000 eggs in her lifetime.

4 The soup slowly turns into a butterfly. When the butterfly wriggles out of the pupa, its wings are soft and creased. They dry in the sunlight.

● Butterflies don't need food to grow, but they love to sip sweet nectar from a flower now and then. It's a fuel that helps them to fly.

How do fish breathe under water?

▷ Not all sea creatures can breathe under water. Sea cows, seals and dolphins breathe air, so they have to keep coming to the surface.

Fish have to breathe to stay alive, just as you do. But while you breathe oxygen from the air, fish take it from water. As they swim, fish gulp in water and push it out through slits called gills on their heads. Oxygen passes from the water into the fish's blood inside their gills.

Gill cover

How do fish swim?

Fish swim by using their muscles to ripple their bodies along. Wiggling their tails from side to side gives them extra push. They use their other fins to balance and change direction.

Which bird flies under water?

Penguins can't fly through the air because their wings are too short and stumpy. They are much more at home in the ocean, where they use their wings as flippers.

Which animal is jet-propelled?

● Seahorses aren't strong swimmers. They hang on to seaweed to avoid being swept away.

Squid don't have flippers or a tail, but they're still fast movers. They suck water into their bodies, then squirt it out so powerfully that their bodies shoot backwards.

● Squid have ten tentacles – that's two more than their relative, the octopus.

Index

This index will help you to find out where you can read information about a subject. It is in alphabetical order. Each section is under a large letter of the alphabet.

A

abdomen 141, 150, 151
Aconcagua, Mount 20
Afghanistan 127
Africa 18, 20, 79, 111, 125, 131
air 24–25, 39, 41, 42, 43, 50, 62, 90
Alaska 126
alligators 142
amphibians 141, 142, 144
Ancient Egyptians 87, 92, 102–103
Ancient Greeks 104–105
Ancient Romans 106–109
animals 21, 49, 50, 124, 125, 138–139, 140–147
Antarctica 18, 20, 123
ants 83
Apatosaurus 98
apes 103, 143
Arabia 111
Arabic 128
archaeologists 108, 109
Archaeopteryx 101
Arctic Ocean 30, 31
Argentina 121
Asia 18, 20, 111
asteroids 14, 15
astronauts 41, 73, 136

astronomers 8, 9, 11, 13
Atlantic Ocean 30, 31, 110
atmosphere 24–25
Australia 18, 20, 111, 121, 131
Austria 121

B

babies 52–53, 59, 140
backbones 55, 144
baking 43
ball-point pens 93
batteries 74
beetles 145
bicycles 36, 91, 127
Big Bang 8
birds 79, 99, 101, 138, 141, 144, 148–149, 155
Biro, Ladislao 93
birth 53
Blackbird 73
blinking 64
blood 53, 58, 59, 67
blood vessels 58
boats 72, 76–77, 104, 126
bodies 52–70
bones 54–55, 56, 57, 67
Boston Tea Party 117
brain 60–61
Brazil 120
breast bone 55
breathing 42, 53, 62, 154
bricks 78
bridges 82–84
Britain 106, 107, 118
bugs 151
buildings 78–84
butterflies 124, 138, 150, 152–153

C

cakes 43
calcium 54
calculators 93
calligraphy 92, 128
Canada 121, 122, 124, 126, 130
cannons 113
carbon dioxide 42, 43
cars 24, 72, 74–75, 90–91
castles 112–113
caterpillars 152–153
cats 49
CD-ROMs 92
centipedes 145, 151
chimpanzees 143
China 111, 120, 122, 127, 128, 132
Chinese New Year 122, 132
chocolate 131
clocks 88–89
clouds 26, 28
coal 87, 118
Cockerell, Christopher 90
coconuts 131
colds 68
Colossus 93
colour 48, 49
Columbus, Christopher 115
combine harvesters 130
comets 14
computers 92–93, 94, 95, 96
conductors 38
continents 18–19
core 17
countries 120–123
crabs 144, 145, 150
cramp 57

crankshafts 75
craters 22
crocodiles 99, 142, 146
crust 17, 22
Crystal Palace 118
cymbals 40

D

damselflies 150
Day of the Dead 135
decks 82
diaphragm 63
diggers 80–81
dinosaurs 96, 98–101
Diwali 133
dizziness 66
dog sleds 126
dolphins 140, 154
dragonflies 150
drawbridges 84, 112
drums 36, 67
dungeons 112
Dutch 129

E

ear drums 67
ears 66–67
Earth 8, 10, 14, 16–19, 24
Ecuador 133
eggs 52, 99, 141, 152, 153
Egypt 102–103, 106
Egyptians, Ancient 87, 92, 102–103
Elasmosaurus 101
elbows 55
Elbrus, Mount 20
electricity 28, 37, 74, 94
elephants 134–135, 138
emus 18
energy 36–39, 40, 44, 74

engines 72, 73, 75, 90, 118
equator 16, 125
Esala Perahera 134–135
Europe 18, 19, 20, 110, 111
Everest, Mount 20, 21, 23
excavators 80
exercise 36, 56
exhaust pipes 74
exoskeletons 145
eyelashes 64
eyes 64–65, 150

F

factories 24, 118
families 118
farming 23, 102, 103, 114, 130–131
faxes 95
feathers 141, 148
feelers 150
felt-tip pens 92
Festival of Light 132
festivals 132–135
fins 141, 154
fire 36
fish 139, 140, 141, 144, 154, 155
fizzy drinks 43
flags 120–121
flies 150
floating and sinking 76
flying 73, 77, 148–149, 155
food 36, 37, 50, 59, 134
Forth Railway Bridge 82
foundations 80, 82
France 104, 106, 116, 120, 129
frisbees 86
frogs 141, 142

funny bones 55

G

galaxies 8–11
gases 12, 35, 42–43
Germany 120
germs 59, 63, 70
gibbons 143
gills 141, 154
giraffes 138
glass 45, 95, 118
glue 86
goats 21
gorillas 143
governments 120
grass 49, 51
grasshoppers 145, 153
Great Exhibition 118
Great Zimbabwe 111, 113
Greece 104–105, 120
Greeks, Ancient 104–105
greenhouse effect 24
gristle 145
grubs 152
guillotine 116
Gunpowder Plot 115

H

hammer bones 67
hang-gliders 39
hares 143
Hawaii 21, 26, 32
head 60
hearing 40
heart 55, 58–59
heat 36, 38, 39
Hebrew 128
hiccups 63
Himalayas 20, 21
Hindi 129
hip bones 55

history 98–118
holes in the ground 80, 82
houses 78–80
hovercraft 77, 90
hoverflies 150–151
human beings 8, 18, 52–70, 139, 140
hummingbirds 148
hydroplanes 72

I

ice 26, 27, 30, 34, 35
Iguanodon 98
illness 70
India 111, 115, 125, 129, 132, 133
Indian Ocean 30, 31
industrial revolution 118
ink 92, 93, 128
insects 59, 141, 143, 144, 145, 150–151, 152–153
inventions 86–87, 118
inventors 86, 87, 96
invertebrates 144, 145
Iraq 79
Ireland 134
iris 64
Israel 120, 128
Italy 104, 106–108

J

Jamaica 121
Japan 92, 111, 126, 128
jaw bone 55
jellyfish 144
jets 73, 90
Jewish New Year 133
Jupiter 14

K

Kentrosaurus 99
Kilimanjaro, Mount 20

Kosciusko, Mount 20

L

languages 128, 129
larvae 152
lava 22
lens 65
leprechauns 134
light 37, 44, 45, 46–47, 48, 49, 50
lightning 28, 29
liquids 34
lizards 99, 146–147
llamas 21
lobsters 145, 150
Loch Ness monster 101
London 84, 106
Louis XVI, King of France 116
lungs 55, 58, 59, 62–63, 140

M

magnifying 47
mammals 140, 143, 144
mantle 17
maps 110–111
Marie Antoinette, Queen of France 116
Mars 14, 15, 23, 136
Mauna Kea 21
mayflies 150
Mayflower 114
McKinley, Mount 20
Mediterranean Sea 33, 103, 104, 111
Mercury 14, 15
metal 17, 38
metamorphosis 152
Mexico 124, 135
Middle Ages 110–111
migration 124

Milky Way 10–11
millipedes 145
mirrors 46, 48
moats 112
money 117, 120
monkeys 131, 143
monsoons 125
Moon 18, 46
moon buggies 73
moons 14
mortar 78
mountains 20–22
movement 36, 37, 56–57
muscles 56–57, 58, 63, 154

N

national anthems 121
nectar 153
Neptune 15
nerves 55, 61, 65, 66, 67, 68, 69
New World 114
New Year 132–133
New Zealand 111, 129
Nile River 102, 103
nitrogen 42
North America 18, 19, 20, 110, 113
nose 63, 68, 145
nymphs 153

O

oceans 30–31, 32
octopus 155
oil 74
Olympus Mons 23
opaque 44
optical fibres 95
orang-utans 143
orbits 15
ostriches 18, 138, 149

Oviraptors 98
oxygen 24, 25, 42, 50, 53, 58, 59, 62, 154
ozone layer 25

P
Pacific Ocean 30, 31, 110
paddy fields 130
Pangaea 18
Panoplosaurus 98
Papua New Guinea 129
penguins 149, 155
penny-farthings 91
periscopes 46
petrol 74, 75
piers 82
Pilgrim Fathers 114–115
pistons 75
planes 23, 25, 73, 90
planets 10, 14–15
plants 44, 50, 51
Pluto 15
Polish 129
Pompeii 106, 108–109
Portugal 126
Post-it notes 86
prawns 144
presidents of USA 117
Proxima Centauri 13
Pueblo Bonito 110, 113
pupa 152–153
pupil 64
pyramids 103
pythons 139

R
rabbits 66, 143
rain 26, 27, 48,125
rainbows 48, 49
rays 44, 47
reading 128
receivers 95

reflection 46
Remus 106
reptiles 99, 100, 141, 142, 144, 146–147
retina 65
ribs 55
rice 130
rock 17, 22
rockets 73
Roman Empire 106–109
Romans 106–109, 110
Rome 106, 107
Romulus 106
Rosh Hashanah 133
rubber 87
Russia 120, 123

S
safety pins 87
sailboards 72
Saint Patrick 134
San Marino 130
Saturn 15
Saudi Arabia 75
science 34–35, 123
scientists 9, 35, 123
scorpions 145
sea 16, 31
sea cows 154
seahorses 155
seals 154
seasons 124–125
seat belts 91
seeing 65
shadows 44–45
Shah Jahan 115
shamrocks 134
sharks 139, 140, 145
sheep 131
ships 76–77, 114
shrimps 150
sieges 112

skeletons 101, 144–145
skiing 73
skin 141, 146–147, 152, 153
skull 55, 60
sky 24, 25
smelling 68
snails 144
snakes 99, 139, 146–147
sneezing 63
snow 27
snowmobiles 126
solar system 14–15
solids 34–35
sounds 36, 40–41, 66–67
South America 18, 20, 110, 131, 133
South Korea 121
Southeast Asia 125, 131
space 41, 136
Spain 106
Spanish 129
spark plugs 75
speaking 69
speed 72–73
sperm 52
spiders 144, 145, 151
Spinosaurus 98
Spirit of Australia 72
squid 145, 155
SR-71A 73
Sri Lanka 134–135
stamps 120
stars 8, 10, 11, 12–13, 15
steam 35, 90, 118
stirrup bones 67
Stygimoloch 98
Styracosaurus 98
submarines 46, 76, 77
Sudan 121
Sun 12–13, 14, 15, 38, 88

sundials 45, 89
sunlight 38, 44, 48
sunspots 12
surfing 32
Swahili 129
Sweden 120
swimming 154, 155

T
Taj Mahal 115
tastebuds 69
tasting 68–69
tears 64
teeth 69
telephones 94–95
temples 102, 103
tendons 57
Thailand 131
Thanksgiving Day 114, 122
thermals 39
thorax 141, 150, 151
Thrust 2 72–73
thunder 29
thunderstorms 28–29
ticking 88
toads 142
tongue 69
tortoises 99
Tower Bridge 84
trains 37, 118, 126
transmitters 95

transparent 45
transport 72–77, 126–127
tropical countries 124–125
trucks 127
trumpets 41
Turkey 104, 121
turtles 146
typewriters 92

U
umbilical cord 53
umbrellas 86
United Kingdom 121
United States of America 84, 95, 114, 117, 122, 130
Universe 8–9
Uranus 15

V
vagina 53
vegetarians 99
Velcro 87
Venus 14
vertebrates 144–145
Vesuvius, Mount 108–109
vibrations 40–41
virtual reality 96
volcanoes 22–23, 108–109

W
Wai-ale-ale, Mount 26
War of Independence 117
Washington, George 117
watches 88
water 34–35, 41, 46, 47, 51, 76
water vapour 35, 42
waves 32
whales 41, 50, 138–139
wheatfields 130
wildebeest 125
wind 42
windpipe 62, 63
wings 141, 148–149, 150–151
womb 52–53
woodlice 143, 150
worms 144
writing 92, 128

Y
yaks 21

Z
zebra 125

Acknowledgements

The publishers would like to thank the following
artists for their contribution to this book:

Susanna Addario, Simone Boni, Peter Cornwell, Joanne Cowne, Peter Dennis, Michael Fisher, Chris Forsey,
Terry Gabbey, Luigi Galante, Ruby Green, Craig Greenwood, Nick Harris, Stephen Holmes, Adam Hook, Christa Hook,
Christian Hook, Biz Hull, Tony Kenyon, Adrian Lascom, Alan Male, Angus McBride, David Mitcheson, Nicki Palin,
Maurice Pledger, Bryan Poole, Sebastian Quigley, Claudia Saraceni, Stephen Seymour, Roger Stewart, Ian Thompson,
Richard Ward, Russ Watton, Linda Worrall, David Wright.